TRAGIC CAVALIER

Governor Manuel Salcedo of Texas, 1808–1813

TRAGIC CAVALIER

Governor Manuel Salcedo of Texas, 1808—1813

By *FÉLIX D. ALMARÁZ, Jr.*

UNIVERSITY OF TEXAS PRESS, AUSTIN & LONDON

Title page drawing by José Cisneros

International Standard Book Number 0–292–70139–x
Library of Congress Catalog Card Number 75–165917
© 1971 by Félix D. Almaráz, Jr.
Printed by The University of Texas Printing Division, Austin
Bound by Universal Bookbindery, Inc., San Antonio

DEDICATED TO MY WIFE

María Olivares Almaráz,

WHOSE LOVE HAS

THE BEAUTY AND FRAGRANCE OF

RED ROSES IN A MISSION GARDEN

CONTENTS

PREFACE

Historians of the Hispanic borderlands generally have surveyed the last years of Spain in North America with uneven emphasis, even if we allow for variety in professional interest and availability of source materials. One example of this tendency is the story of Texas in the early nineteenth century. After decades of official neglect, the province was at that time a buffer area, which upholders of Spanish rule could not adequately defend against the pressures of westward expansionists from the Mississippi Valley and the thrusts of insurrectionists from the lower Rio Grande Valley. This period of Texas' two decades of unrest, decline, and collapse has not been especially attractive to scholars, who have preferred to study the borderlands in terms of defensive expansion under the impetus of the Bourbon reformers.

Understandably, study of the breakdown of Spanish rule in the northern provinces offers a certain pitfall that some historians try to avoid: offending the successors to the government of New Spain. Perhaps this is one reason why specialists of nineteenth-century Hispanic Texas have hurriedly pushed through their material to arrive at the safe haven of 1821. Even the late, eminent Carlos Eduardo Castañeda, in the fifth volume of his monumental *Our Catholic Heritage in Texas*, succumbed to this temptation. As a result, Hispanic guardians who fought to defend a tottering colonial structure have been depicted as antiquated and reactionary, as obstacles in the path of a new social order.

Manuel María de Salcedo, governor of Spanish Texas from November, 1808, to April, 1813, is a representative example of extreme assessment. Castañeda, at his best, described Salcedo as a "loyal and gallant" royalist who exerted himself "to the utmost in defending the remote Province of Texas." Odie B. Faulk, in sharp contrast, assessed Don Manuel as "a rather weak governor during an extremely critical period in the history of Spanish Texas." Walter Prescott Webb's cooperative venture, *The Handbook of Texas*, summarized the major aspects of Salcedo's administration as futile and unsuccessful. Conversely, Virginia Houston Taylor, translator and editor of the correspondence of another governor who served Texas during the transition period from Spanish to Mexican rule, credited Salcedo as being "an able, energetic, and educated man."

With the notable exception of Nettie Lee Benson, some writers who have expressed an affinity for the Hispanic culture—like Vito Alessio Robles, J. Villasana Haggard, and Luis Navarro García—were concerned with historical themes other than the careers of borderlanders who upheld the royalist tradition. Still another group of historians, such as Julia Kathryn Garrett, Walter Flavius McCaleb, Harris Gaylord Warren, and Henderson R. Yoakum, apart from recognizing that Salcedo's rule coincided with the outbreak of the revolt of Padre Miguel Hidalgo, concentrated attention on movements that overwhelmed the Spanish provincial government. Thus an appraisal of Salcedo's stewardship in Texas has been difficult, but not altogether impossible, to construct. *Tragic Cavalier*, the culmination of a long endeavor, is a historical account of the Mexican independence movement in Texas as seen from the Spanish point of view.

For contributing to the research project in numerous and distinct ways, the writer is principally indebted to the following persons: Dr. Donald C. Cutter, of The University of New Mexico, for directing the research and writing effort from its inception as a dissertation problem in 1965 to its submission in the Popejoy Dissertation Award competition in 1968, and for manifesting a sincere interest in the professional growth and advancement of his disciples; Dr. Michael E. Thurman, formerly of Southern Methodist University, for his wise counsel and genuine friendship during Professor Cutter's sabbatical leave in 1966; Dr. Frank C. Stuart, now at the University of Miami, for accepting me as a partner in college instruction, all of which made my assignment as his graduate assistant in 1964–1965 a memorable and rewarding experience; Dr. Chester V. Kielman, archivist of The University of Texas at Austin, for his help and cooperation in the use of the Béxar Archives; Dr. Hubert J. Miller, former chairman of the Department of History, St. Mary's University of San Antonio, for arranging an equitable teaching schedule in 1967–1968 to assure the completion of the writing task; Professor Harl A. Dalstrom, of the University of Nebraska at Omaha, for inviting me to deliver a paper, "Governor Manuel de Salcedo of Hispanic Texas, 1808–1813—A Reappraisal," at the Eleventh Missouri Valley Conference of Collegiate Teachers of History (now known as the Missouri Valley History Conference) in March, 1968; Congressman Henry B. González, of Texas' Twentieth Congressional District, for establishing fruitful contact with the National Archives in Washington, D.C.; Mr. Richard G. Santos, former archivist of Bexar County, for making available special materials in his private collection; Mrs. Mary Lynn Kilday, my student assistant in 1967–1968, for managing the office routine and typing lecture notes; Mr. Robert E. Davis, of Texian Press in Waco, for granting permission to incorporate material from my article on Salcedo that he published in *Texana* (Spring, 1968); Master Sergeant Thomas M. Hardgrave, USAF, for duplicating copies of the manuscript for submission in the Presidio La Bahía Award competition in 1969; and Señor José Cisneros of El Paso, a friend and extremely gifted artist, for providing the drawing for the title page.

In a deep and personal sense, I give full credit to my wife, María, for loyal, loving, and devoted support, especially during the bleak years of graduate study when the hours were long, the disappointments were many, and the rewards were so elusive. It is certain that without her encouragement, particularly in the final months of writing and revision, this humble contribution to Southwestern Americana would not have materialized. The result definitely has been a family project, one that began in the upper Rio Grande Valley of New Mexico and terminated in the lower Rio Grande Valley of Texas. Of course, the author gracefully assumes responsibility for all omissions and shortcomings.

TRAGIC CAVALIER

Governor Manuel Salcedo of Texas, 1808–1813

1. HISPANIC TEXAS AT THE BEGINNING OF THE NINETEENTH CENTURY: *A Survey*

Spanish Texas at the beginning of the nineteenth century was a neglected frontier area entrusted by officialdom with the task of safeguarding the empire from disintegration. No northern province in far-flung New Spain received less attention in time of peace and more demands in time of crisis than Texas. For over two centuries after Pineda sighted the coast of the region in 1519, Spain ignored the area, content merely to claim it, except when covetous designs of foreigners prompted the government into action—first to expel the invaders and then to initiate token missionary and colonization efforts to hold Texas in the name of the king. It was almost axiomatic that, whenever external forces threatened the periphery of the empire in the north, Spain moved with grandeur and determination, only to relax the vigilance when the danger subsided. Accordingly, colonial Texas, created to thwart alien encroachment, retained an international importance as a defensive outpost.[1]

The history of Texas as a Hispanic borderland was one of shifting emphasis influenced by outside events, mostly European in origin.[2] As the eighteenth century closed, Spain clearly had overreached herself in the northern provinces; of these, Texas, in the estimate of one knowledgeable official, was "the 'key to all New Spain.' "[3] Even so, Hispanic Texans, despite frontier hardships, submissively basked in the afterglow of the glory once enjoyed by the empire and maintained a prosaic existence that offered little, promised nothing, and resisted change.

As the nineteenth century unfolded, the remnants of Spanish imperial greatness in Texas consisted of three principal settlements connected by a highway system impressively called the Camino Real, a few presidios, and a score of weather-eroded missions.[4] Geographically, the boundaries of the province were indefinite, but through widespread acceptance the inhabitants recognized the "general limits" charted on a royal map filed in 1805 and by an administrative order of May 1, 1811.[5] These documents described the Nueces River—from its mouth to the junction with Moros Creek—as the southwestern boundary. From this interior point, the line that formed the northern edge of the province extended in an arc to the Medina River and then in an irregular, sometimes staggered, easterly course to the Red

---

[1] Herbert Eugene Bolton, "Defensive Spanish Expansion and Significance of the Borderlands," in *Bolton and the Spanish Borderlands*, ed. John Francis Bannon, p. 51.

[2] Sidney B. Brinckerhoff and Odie B. Faulk, *Lancers for the King: A Study of the Frontier Military System of Northern New Spain*, p. 85.

[3] Julia Kathryn Garrett, *Green Flag over Texas: A Story of the Last Years of Spain in Texas*, p. 3.

[4] *Ibid.*

[5] William Campbell Binkley, *The Expansionist Movement in Texas, 1826–1850*, pp. 7–8.

River.[6] A more precise terminal, even though the southwestern limits of Louisiana were vague in the initial years of the nineteenth century, was the Sabine River, the eastern border of Texas. Finally, on the south, the Gulf of Mexico served as an immovable margin,[7] completing the boundaries of the Hispanic domain that for over a century had "stood guard successfully against the French, the British, and the United States."[8] For such faithful service, Spanish Texans received no tangible rewards (except troops and armaments), only unceasing demands to remain loyal to God and monarch and to keep out aggressive intruders who possessed enticing goods and subversive ideas.[9]

Of the three chief population centers, the capital was the most important in terms of geography and provincial politics. Officially named Villa de San Fernando at the time of its founding in 1731, the civil settlement through common usage gradually assumed the name of the military establishment within its confines, Presidio San Antonio de Béxar—to the confusion of fastidious administrators.[10] Most settlers, however, uninhibited

[6] *Ibid.*

[7] Norman C. Guice (ed. and trans.), "Texas in 1804," *Southwestern Historical Quarterly*, 59, no. 1 (July, 1955), 48.

[8] Garrett, *Green Flag over Texas*, p. 3.

[9] Hubert Howe Bancroft, *History of the North Mexican States and Texas*, II, 8–9, 11; Frank W. Johnson, *A History of Texas and Texans*, ed. Eugene C. Barker and Ernest William Winkler, I, 5; Walter Prescott Webb, *The Texas Rangers: A Century of Frontier Defense*, pp. 9–10; R. Woods Moore, "The Role of the Baron de Bastrop in the Anglo-American Settlement of the Spanish Southwest," *Louisiana Historical Quarterly*, 31, no. 3 (July, 1948), 632–633. Philip Nolan and Peter Ellis Bean were prototypes of the first aggressive interlopers who trespassed into Spanish territory, ostensibly to catch wild horses but more plausibly to survey the possibilities of trade and to appraise the strength of imperial defenses. Among the foreigners who gained entrance through peaceful and legal means, by swearing allegiance to Spanish sovereignty and Catholicism, were Samuel Davenport, Robert Barr, and the Baron de Bastrop.

[10] Popular opinion notwithstanding, in 1809, as a result of much confusion, Governor Manuel María de Salcedo proclaimed that all official correspond-

by subtle distinctions, regarded the two communities and their environs as one compact unit and referred to it simply as Béxar, the name that to them seemed more appropriate.[11] Be that as it may, the capital, situated "on the very fertile banks" of the San Antonio River, contained a population of "2,500 souls, including the troops."[12] In spite of the growth of the colony from mission site to provincial capital,[13] not every individual, transient or native, appreciated the rate of progress, obviously slow by later standards. One visitor in 1777 and 1778, Fray Juan Agustín Morfi, chaplain of Commandant General Teodoro de Croix, caustically observed:

On the west bank of the San Antonio river, about a league from its source, above the point where San Pedro creek joins the river, is situated the villa of San Fernando and the presidio of San Antonio de Béxar, with no other division between them than the parochial

---

ence, particularly legal documents, would bear the name of the Villa de San Fernando de Béxar, reflecting the increased importance of the civil community over the military post. (Carlos E. Castañeda, *Our Catholic Heritage in Texas, 1519–1936,* V, 411).

[11] Frank W. Blackmar, *Spanish Institutions of the Southwest,* p. 231; Maury Maverick (cooperating sponsor), *Old Villita,* p. 9; Sister Mary Angela Fitzmorris, *Four Decades of Catholicism in Texas, 1820–1860,* p. 3.

[12] Odie Faulk (ed. and trans.), "A Description of Texas in 1803," *Southwestern Historical Quarterly,* 56, no. 4 (April, 1963), 513.

[13] In 1718, twelve years before the founding of the civil settlement Villa de San Fernando, Martín de Alarcón, governor of Coahuila and Texas, recognized the need of having a "half way station between Mexico and the East Texas missions" and established a mission, San Antonio de Valero, on the east side of the San Antonio River and a presidio, San Antonio de Béxar, on the west side of the stream (Birch Duke Kimbrough, "The Spanish Regime in Texas" [Master's thesis, East Texas State Teachers College, 1939], p. 13). In response to a thorough inspection of the northern provinces by the Marqués de Rubí, deputy of royal Visitador José de Gálvez, the viceregal government in 1772 transferred the capital from Los Adaes in East Texas to San Antonio (Juan Agustín Morfi, *History of Texas, 1673–1779,* trans. Carlos Eduardo Castañeda, II, 419).

church. . . . The church building is spacious and has a vaulted roof, but the whole [building] is so poorly constructed that it promises but a short life. The town consists of fifty-nine houses of stone and mud and seventy-nine of wood, but all poorly built, without any preconceived plan, so that the whole [community] resembles more a poor village than a villa, capital of so pleasing a province. . . . The soldiers' quarters, originally built of stone and adobe, are almost in ruins. . . . The streets are tortuous and are filled with mud the minute it rains. The presidio is surrounded by a poor stockade on which are mounted a few swivel guns, without shelter or defense, that can be used only for firing a salvo.[14]

Ten years later another visitor, an associate of Pedro Vial, the peripatetic frontiersman of French descent who served the Spanish government in the Louisiana–Texas–New Mexico salient, noted some improvement in the capital, especially in the dwellings: some were "of rubble work, but more . . . [being] of wood of moderate structure."[15] A still later observer was Zebulon M. Pike, an uninvited wanderer who, while being escorted out of Spanish lands in 1807, passed through San Antonio. Afterwards he recorded that "St. Antonio . . . contains perhaps 2,000 souls, most of whom reside in miserable mudwall houses, covered with thatched grass roofs. The town is laid out on a very grand plan."[16] However, probably recalling courtesies extended to him in Texas, Pike admitted that "St. Antonio [is] one of the most agreeable places that we met with in the [Spanish] provinces."[17]

Its location at the center of the province undoubtedly made San Antonio "one of the most agreeable places." Aside from polit-

[14] Morfi, *History of Texas*, I, 92–93.

[15] Noel M. Loomis and Abraham P. Nasatir, *Pedro Vial and the Roads to Santa Fe*, p. 356.

[16] Elliott Coues (ed.), *The Expeditions of Zebulon Montgomery Pike, to Headwaters of the Mississippi River, through Louisiana Territory, and in New Spain, during the Years 1805–6–7*, II, 783–784.

[17] *Ibid.*, II, 785–786.

ical considerations, the settlers enjoyed "the purity of its air," a feature that prompted one Latin American in Spain to report that Texas' "climate is very healthful, though the sun is very hot in the summer and snows are common in the winter."[18] Certainly the healthful climate and the availability of water, in addition to the willingness of Indians to submit to mission life, contributed to the success of the missionaries in the San Antonio area. (Although partly secularized in 1793, the mission establishments, in descending order down the river away from the civil settlement, included San Antonio de Valero, La Purísima Concepción de Acuña, San José de Aguayo, San Juan Capistrano, and San Francisco de la Espada.)[19]

San Antonio de Béxar, as the capital of the province, was the governor's official residence.[20] Following the transfer of the seat of authority from East Texas in 1772, the chief royal administrator, for lack of proper quarters, temporarily stayed at the local jail, which one observer described as "a poor residence at best."[21] Eventually the government provided the Texas executive with adequate facilities, built on the east side of the military plaza, pretentiously called the Casas Reales.[22]

Adjacent to the main settlement but separated by the river was a small village in which were located the homes of married

[18] Nettie Lee Benson (ed. and trans.), *Report that Dr. Miguel Ramos de Arizpe Priest of Borbon, and Deputy in the Present General and Special Cortes of Spain for the Province of Coahuila One of the Four Eastern Interior Provinces of the Kingdom of Mexico Presents to the August Congress on the Natural, Political and Civil Condition of the Provinces of Coahuila, Nuevo León, Nuevo Santander, and Texas of the Four Eastern Interior Provinces of the Kingdom of Mexico*, p. 6. Hereinafter cited as *Arizpe Report*.

[19] Kimbrough, "The Spanish Regime in Texas," p. 45; Guice, "Texas in 1804," pp. 47–48.

[20] Morfi, *History of Texas*, I, 79.

[21] *Ibid.*, I, 93.

[22] Richard G. Santos, "The Quartel de San Antonio de Bexar," *Texana*, 5, no. 3 (Fall, 1967), 189.

presidial soldiers, older families who originally had been attached to Mission San Antonio de Valero before its seculariza-
tion, and some settlers who had fled from East Texas before the
close of the eighteenth century.[23] Altogether, the residents of
La Villita comprised an element of society that lived on "the
wrong side of the river."[24] One reliable authority wrote:

Villita, meaning little town, was settled by some of the soldiers who
came with the [Spanish] . . . Army and those who had intermarried
with Indians, and who were not supposed to be of the very best
people. In fact there was a great distinction between the east and
west side of the river. The west side . . . was supposed to be the residence of the first families [the Canary Islanders] . . . and the
descendants of the Indians and the Spanish soldiers settled on the
east side of the river.[25]

Independent of the social implications, by 1800 the Villita families, inspired by the normal expansion of the larger villa,
ignored the discriminations of the *isleños* and became plain
"citizens of Bexar."[26]

At the river's edge of the "little town" was the "principal ford
for wagons and riders on horseback." Pedestrians, by choice or
necessity, walked across a public log, often missing after a flood,
which was placed at "the narrowest part of the stream."[27] A
traveler arriving in San Antonio by way of the suburban village,
on traversing the river,

entered at once into the City of San Fernando and the first street
[extending east and west], . . . was the main thoroughfare. There
was just one more street to the north [of the main street and called

---

[23] Maverick, *Old Villita*, p. 9.
[24] *Ibid.*, p. 8.
[25] [J. María Rodríguez], *Rodriguez Memoirs of Early Texas*, pp. 37–38.
[26] Maverick, *Old Villita*, p. 9.
[27] Robert Sturmberg (comp.), *History of San Antonio and of the Early
Days in Texas*, pp. 51–52.

El Potrero, meaning herdsman of colts[28]]: . . . Houses were built closely together; they all were of the one-story kind and topped with flat roofs. This construction was the only practical one for warding off the attacks of savage Indians. . . . After barricading doors and windows the defenders fought the Indians from the top of their houses, retreating and advancing over them as the case might be.[29]

Although San Antonio de Béxar represented the most vital population center, downriver, about forty leagues southeast from the capital, was the coastal settlement of La Bahía del Espíritu Santo. Another presidio-mission complex of strategic importance to the security of the province, La Bahía had approximately six hundred inhabitants.[30] This fortification, explained by military urgency, included "a long building for official quarters, . . . a guard house," and a "well-built stone church." Located near the presidio were three deteriorated missions, one of which sheltered about two hundred Indians.[31] The settlers at La Bahía, less fortunate than those at Béxar, annually experienced crop failures due to a shortage of irrigation water; as a result, they depended heavily on the generosity of the capital dwellers.[32]

The third settlement, Nacogdoches, twenty leagues west of the Sabine River in the piney woods of East Texas, stood as a lonely "sentinel of Spanish sovereignty." Largely an outgrowth of an Indian mission built in 1716, Nacogdoches at the beginning of the nineteenth century consisted of a stone fortress around which clustered "a village of log houses."[33] The fortification itself

[28] Auguste Frételliere, "Adventures of a Castrovillian," in Julia Nott Waugh, *Castro-Ville and Henry Castro*, p. 91.

[29] Sturmberg, *History of San Antonio*, pp. 51–52.

[30] Faulk, "Texas in 1803," p. 514.

[31] Garrett, *Green Flag over Texas*, p. 6.

[32] Faulk, "Texas in 1803," p. 514.

[33] Garrett, *Green Flag over Texas*, pp. 6–7.

was twenty feet tall, twenty feet six inches wide, and seventy feet long. The fort had solid walnut beam-floors, and the wall partitions were of adobe brick. The outside double doors were heavy and made out of durable oak. It was a typical frontier building, having a rambling two story structure, made of native stone, and the roof was peaked and shingled with thick boards. The roof also had two chimneys. This building had a twenty foot, two-decked gallery or porch, running its full length, upheld by spindly, hand-sewn columns. The walls were built oblong.[34]

The population of this border area varied because of clandestine movements in both directions across the Sabine, but in 1803 it totalled "770 souls."[35] Many of these, evidently tempted by the proximity of foreign soil and the concealment offered by the wooded terrain, were apathetic soldiers, disloyal traders, and possibly even law-breakers actively engaged in illicit trading of livestock, hides, and wool in nearby Louisiana.[36]

These three centers, connected by the Camino Real, or the King's Highway, constituted all that remained of Spanish imperialism in Texas. The highway served as a vital link by which Hispanic Texans maintained contact with Mexico City, the center of the viceroyalty. Emanating from Monclova, the road traversed the Rio Grande at Presidio del Rio Grande, cut through a mesquite-covered area to San Antonio, then moved on to Nacogdoches, and finally terminated at the Anglo-American outpost of Natchitoches. Another highway, less frequented but surely important, started at the presidio of Laredo at the Rio Grande, crossed directly to La Bahía, then turned northeast and intersected the upper road at Trinity Crossing.[37]

[34] Nyal C. King, "Captain Antonio Gil Y'Barbo: Founder of Modern Nacogdoches, 1729–1809" (Master's thesis, Stephen F. Austin State Teachers College, 1949), p. 60.
[35] Faulk, "Texas in 1803," pp. 514–515.
[36] Garrett, *Green Flag over Texas*, p. 7.
[37] *Ibid.*

South of the upper highway dwelled seminomadic Indian
tribes who confined their activities mostly to hunting and fishing.
Of necessity, they migrated northward once a year "to provide
themselves with buffalo and bear meat." Despite the efforts of
missionaries, these Indian groups, generally not dangerous to
provincial stability, preferred to limit their contact with Chris-
tianity to material benefits. North of the road, however, roamed
hostile bands, principally Comanches, who periodically raided
the settlements.[38] Such bold attacks, clearly an affront to Spanish
arms, painfully convinced royal officials that the mission-presidio
system, effective elsewhere, did not function north of San Antonio de Béxar.[39] Frontiersmen persistently requested a new approach to the frustrating problem.

To correct the failure of "the old system," at least in Hispanic
Texas, the government fluctuated from a policy of retaliation to
one of peace, depending on conditions and resources, until it re-
luctantly adopted a method used successfully by the French,
"distributing presents and . . . granting special trade privileges to
the Indians."[40] Regrettably, the French technique as imitated by
the Spaniards became an expensive operation that could not be
consistently supported. Not surprisingly, the recipients grew
restless and unfriendly as goods were reduced and curtailed.[41] To
complicate the Indian question for colonial administrators even
further, Anglo-Americans, early in the nineteenth century,
stealthily "began to enter the Comanche villages to trade." In the
eyes of Spanish defenders of the borderlands, these unauthorized

---

[38] *Arizpe Report*, p. 7; Rupert Norval Richardson, *The Comanche Barrier
to South Plains Settlement: A Century and a Half of Savage Resistance to the
Advancing White Frontier*, pp. 69–70.

[39] Herbert Eugene Bolton, *Texas in the Middle Eighteenth Century: Studies
in Spanish Colonial History and Administration*, p. 380; Rupert Norval Richardson, *Texas: The Lone Star State*, p. 36.

[40] Kimbrough, "The Spanish Regime in Texas," p. 52.

[41] *Ibid.*

intrusions presented "a serious threat to the peace and order of the provinces."[42] Collectively, these two problems—the Indian menace and foreign penetration—complicated the affairs of civil and military governors in Texas until the end of Spain's rule in North America.

In a broad sense the government of Texas was "a military despotism." Although no Spanish sovereign had ever visited his American colonies, the king, as a symbol of personalism, wielded considerable power, albeit indirectly, in the remotest provinces of his empire, including the Texan wilderness. The royal flag of resplendent red and gold, for example, that waved conspicuously over the governor's residence reminded capital inhabitants and visitors of "his sovereignty." Most Hispanic Texans, to be sure, never saw their monarch, but they understood that imperial will and prerogative stemmed from the governor of the province, a person whom they obeyed, respected, and perhaps even feared. The governor's colorful "accouterments and dwelling in Béxar symbolized the omnipotence of His Majesty in Spain." As the king's leading representative in the frontier, the governor administered a multitude of responsibilities ranging from military affairs and Indian relations to matters of jurisprudence and civil government.[43] One function for which the colonial executive was not accountable, however, was the spiritual welfare of the province, a responsibility exercised by the bishop of Nuevo León. To carry out this obligation of administering the religious needs of the faithful in Texas, the bishop assigned parish priests to San Antonio de Béxar and La Bahía and Franciscan padres to the missions and Nacogdoches.[44]

All-encompassing as the gubernatorial powers appeared at first

[42] Richardson, *The Comanche Barrier to South Plains Settlement*, pp. 72–73.

[43] Garrett, *Green Flag over Texas*, pp. 7–8.

[44] *Arizpe Report*, p. 12.

glance, save for ecclesiastical questions, the governor performed his duties under the direct supervision of the commandant general of the Interior Provinces, whose headquarters were in the city of Chihuahua.[45] Created in 1776 to strengthen New Spain's defenses in the north, the commandancy general underwent several reorganizations,[46] until ultimately, by authority of a royal decree of November 24, 1792, it included the provinces of Sonora, Chihuahua, Nueva Vizcaya, Nuevo México, Coahuila, and Texas.[47] Under this restructuring, the commandant general was absolved of every responsibility to the viceregal government,[48] except that of prudent consultation, and ruled in the king's name over an immense vastness measuring approximately 59,375 square leagues and extending from the Pacific Ocean to the Sabine River, within which were mountains, deserts, and prairies. Unmanageable as the supervisory task appeared, the commandant general nonetheless directed the governors who served under him in the six provinces. From his office in Chihuahua, the senior officer

planned defense, studied the unconquerable problem of Indian hostilities and Indian trade, and pondered over the dangers to his realm arising from intruding American traders and the greed of the United States. He wrote letters full of instructions for the six governors; kept couriers laboriously riding the hundreds of leagues from Chihuahua to the capitals of the provinces; prepared detailed reports for His Majesty; and sent information to Mexico City, . . . to another of the king's representatives—the viceroy of New Spain.[49]

[45] Bancroft, *History of the North Mexican States and Texas*, II, 4.

[46] Charles F. Coan, *A History of New Mexico*, I, 251–252.

[47] Luis Navarro García, *Don José de Gálvez y la Comandancia General de las Provincias Internas del Norte de Nueva España*, p. 486.

[48] Coan, *A History of New Mexico*, I, 252.

[49] Garrett, *Green Flag over Texas*, pp. 8–9.

Obviously, the discharge of such comprehensive duties called for initiative, imagination, and finances, requisites Spain critically lacked in sufficient quantity to meet the challenge of repeated crises in the nineteenth century. Nonetheless, whenever the royal treasury permitted, the commandant general assisted his subordinate officers, especially the governor of Texas—if not continually with guns and troops, then with decrees and reprimands, but seldom with commendations.

Even as a subordinate official subject to superior orders from Chihuahua, the Texas governor, at times left to his own resources, performed duties that were definitely within his sphere of authority. For instance, as military commander he appointed lieutenants, always dependent on his will, to command the cavalry units at La Bahía and Nacogdoches. To oversee the mission settlements, obviously not as important as the larger centers but worthy of token surveillance, he assigned corporals.[50] In his capacity as civil administrator, the governor generally respected the royal charter that granted to the inhabitants of San Antonio de Béxar a semblance of local autonomy,[51] but he reserved the right to review all decisions affecting the municipality.[52] In particular, "he had to approve all elections made by the *ayuntamiento*, and, although his approval was usually given, the elections were null if it was withheld. In addition . . . he, or his representatives, had to install all new officers. Furthermore, he might preside over the *ayuntamiento* if he so desired, and could cast the deciding vote in case of a tie in the election of officers."[53] Under such restrictions, the *cabildo* of San Antonio de Béxar, the

[50] *Arizpe Report*, p. 10.

[51] Margaret Miller, "Survey of Civil Government of San Antonio, Texas, 1731–1948" (Master's thesis, St. Mary's University, 1948), p. 15.

[52] Dick Smith, "The Development of Local Government Units in Texas" (Ph.D. dissertation, Harvard University, 1938), p. 8.

[53] *Ibid.*

lowest echelon of the "political hierarchy" of Spanish officialdom, mainly carried out "the orders of the higher authorities."[54]

The municipal government initially consisted of two *alcaldes* (judges), one *procurador* (attorney), and six *regidores* (aldermen), all elected annually,[55] but in 1807 the governor was directed by his superiors either to abolish the town council or to reduce its membership. He decided, possibly in deference to the prestige of the provincial capital, to reduce only the number of aldermen by two-thirds.[56] Undaunted by the shortage of four members, the town council, dominated by the descendants of the *isleño* aristocracy, continued to aid the governor in his administration of the capital. He permitted them to enact ordinances dealing with "sanitation, hospitals, charity, schools, and policing the villa."[57]

Advanced as the provincial government of Texas seemed in relation to domestic issues, in an international crisis it was virtually disabled unless sustained from the center of the Interior Provinces. Illustrative of this disability was the reaction precipitated in 1803 by the French cession of Louisiana to the United States, an event that rocked the Spanish empire from Madrid to Mexico City and caused repercussions to be felt from Chihuahua to San Antonio de Béxar.

The crisis on the Texas-Louisiana frontier forced the commandant general to take prompt steps to close the borders to undesirable elements. Only loyal Spanish subjects in Louisiana who indicated a genuine desire to relocate in Texas were allowed

[54] Mattie Alice Austin, "The Municipal Government of San Fernando de Bexar, 1739–1800," *Quarterly of the Texas State Historical Association*, 8, no. 4 (April, 1905), 307.

[55] Vito Alessio Robles, *Coahuila y Texas en la época colonial*, p. 611.

[56] Nettie Lee Benson, "Texas Failure to Send a Deputy to the Spanish Cortes, 1810–1812," *Southwestern Historical Quarterly*, 64, no. 1 (July, 1960), 23 n. 25.

[57] Garrett, *Green Flag over Texas*, p. 8.

to enter, provided they settled far away from their former habitats "to prevent contraband practices."[58] Undoubtedly the undefined western boundary of Louisiana aggravated matters, a problem that required diplomatic resolution at higher levels, but the commandant general, faced with a graver problem of defending the empire in the north, seldom yielded to protocol in an emergency.

The presence of Anglo-Americans on the threshold of Spanish dominions understandably created tension on the eastern borderland. The matter came to a head when the United States assembled troops near the Sabine River; such armed movements constituted a definite danger, in the opinion of Spanish officials. In 1805, when the governor of Texas, incapacitated by illness, appealed for immediate assistance with which to meet the challenge, the commandant general responded by dispatching the governor of Coahuila in command of a force of three hundred men to guard East Texas.[59] Moreover, from neighboring provinces outside of his jurisdiction the commandant general obtained a contingent of seven hundred militiamen to support the special troops in Texas.[60] In 1805 and 1806 Hispanic Texans unknowingly witnessed the last display of imperial military might against a foreign power, like a dying person desperately struggling for survival.

Fortunately for both sides, the end result was not a clash of arms, but a negotiated settlement by which the respective commanders on their own initiative informally created a demilitarized zone, called the Neutral Ground, between the Sabine River

---

[58] Isaac Joslin Cox, "The Louisiana-Texas Frontier," *Southwestern Historical Quarterly*, 17, no. 1 (July, 1913), 33.

[59] Isaac Joslin Cox, "The Louisiana-Texas Frontier during the Burr Conspiracy," *Mississippi Valley Historical Review*, 10, no. 3 (December, 1923), 277.

[60] *Arizpe Report*, p. 11.

and the Arroyo Hondo in Louisiana.[61] Tacitly sanctioned by the governments of both nations, this agreement remained in effect until 1819, when a more permanent treaty defined the boundary between Texas and Louisiana.[62] Clearly, the Neutral Ground solution removed the immediate threat of war, but Spanish officials, though they returned to more normal pursuits, continually kept a watchful eye on what took place in the piney woods of East Texas.

Evidently the "bustle of arms" had a positive impact on the economic life of the province, but any prosperity was probably short-lived because Hispanic Texans in general ignored the "extra-ordinary and profitable resources"[63] and concentrated on agriculture and stock-raising. Accordingly, although Texas farm produce fell appreciably behind the rate of production in Coahuila and Nuevo León, the colonists enjoyed "some progress,"[64] enough to sustain life on the frontier but certainly not in the great abundance necessary to constitute an export economy. Mainly because of natural setbacks, Texas' principal crops were limited "to the sowing of corn, a little wheat, and less sugar cane in the vicinity of San Antonio de Véjar [sic] and La Bahía."[65] In addition to the cultivation of corn, some individuals planted beans and chili peppers, but only "enough for their annual main-

[61] J. Villasana Haggard, "The Neutral Ground between Louisiana and Texas, 1806–1821," *Louisiana Historical Quarterly*, 28, no. 4 (October, 1945), 1043; Charles Carroll Griffin, *The United States and the Disruption of the Spanish Empire, 1810–1822: A Study of the Relations of the United States with Spain and with the Rebel Spanish Colonies*, p. 25.

[62] J. Villasana Haggard, "The Counter-Revolution in Béxar, 1811," *Southwestern Historical Quarterly*, 43, no. 2 (October, 1939), 235. Simón de Herrera, the Spanish commander, and James Wilkinson, the American general, were the principal officers who on November 6, 1806, entered into the Neutral Ground agreement.

[63] *Arizpe Report*, p. 21.

[64] *Ibid.*, p. 18.

[65] *Ibid.*

tenance."[66] Indeed, those persons inclined to cultivate the soil seemed to have been more motivated by utter necessity than by pride in their work. Very few farmers, for instance, engaged in cotton production, an effort that yielded "about 300 pounds of a very good quality."[67] Settlers at La Bahía, lacking an adequate irrigation system, experienced so many crop failures that they often asked San Antonio inhabitants to send corn supplies to them. At Nacogdoches, on the other hand, frequent floods destroyed the crops. Under these dire circumstances, Spanish frontiersmen would have nearly starved if they had not slaughtered wild cattle and fowl "at proper seasons" to supplement their meager diet.[68]

Apart from these narrow agricultural endeavors, the main interest among Spanish colonists was livestock breeding, which unquestionably "became the largest single industry in the province."[69] In the first half of the eighteenth century, thousands, possibly even millions, of wild cattle and horses roamed the Texas plains. Throughout this period mounted hunters indiscriminately destroyed untamed cattle until the herds dwindled to an alarming scarcity.[70] Even reduced, however, livestock raising formed the economic base of Texas.

Cattle ranches in the province were most numerous from San Antonio southward to La Bahía . . . This area was covered with individuals holding large grants and raising stock. At Nacogdoches there were a few horse ranches, as well as many for cattle. This locality was far enough to the east that the plains raiders [Indians] were unlikely to disturb them. And at each of the missions still extant,

---

[66] Faulk, "Texas in 1803," p. 513.
[67] Guice, "Texas in 1804," pp. 53–54.
[68] Garrett, *Green Flag over Texas*, pp. 9–10.
[69] Odie B. Faulk, "Ranching in Spanish Texas," *Hispanic American Historical Review*, 45, no. 2 (May, 1965), 262.
[70] Alessio Robles, *Coahuila y Texas*, pp. 607–608.

large herds were kept, constituting the greatest source of income for
the Franciscans.[71]

While ranching appeared fairly well developed, if confined
mostly to the principal population centers, industry and manu-
facturing were retarded. Texas merchants realized that surplus
agricultural products and finished goods were practically worth-
less if they could not be exchanged for something else. Specifically, they complained, though not too vociferously, that Spain's
stringent economic policy denied them an opportunity to stage a
commercial fair at which excess wares might be traded, or the
privilege of trading through any of the province's "numerous
ports" or even with Natchitoches, the nearest Anglo-American
outpost.[72] Such discriminating restrictions forced the few merchants in Texas "to sell raw products in the Saltillo Fair in Coahuila . . . receiving them again manufactured at four times their
[original] value."[73] Moreover, since all finished goods allowed
into New Spain first entered through Veracruz, the Texas con-
sumer "bore the burden of freights, duties, and profits of the
merchants of Cadiz, Vera Cruz, Saltillo, and the local Texas re-
tailer."[74] Thus, it was not surprising that "excessive prices and
distant markets" completely retarded industry in Spanish Texas
and restricted "profitable agriculture" to the cultivation of essential crops.[75]

In view of the conditions in Texas in the first decade of the
nineteenth century, few Hispanic frontiersmen doubted that the
province, still loyal after nearly a century of neglect, could remain indifferent to the crosswinds of change, a slight breeze from
across the Rio Grande and a stronger gust from over the Sabine.

[71] Faulk, "Ranching in Spanish Texas," p. 263.
[72] Garrett, *Green Flag over Texas*, pp. 9–10.
[73] *Ibid.*
[74] *Ibid.*
[75] *Ibid.*

Some knowledgeable officials, such as the one who observed that Texas was "the 'key to all New Spain,' " correctly assessed the situation by advising that the kingdom would be lost unless Spain introduced widespread reforms for the borderlands. But, exhausted by tremendous expenditures and disappointments of global politics and frightened of the future, the home government regrettably decided in favor of a remedial holding action, a policy of stresses and strains that eventually failed to safeguard the empire from disintegration. Such were the precarious conditions in Hispanic Texas when Manuel María de Salcedo arrived in 1808 to assume his post as governor of the province. Little did he realize, as he entered Texas from Louisiana, that his administration would be characterized by rebellion and personal tragedy.

2. SALCEDO'S INITIAL YEAR IN
TEXAS: *A Division of Authority*

IN EARLY SEPTEMBER, 1808, a group of travel-weary Spaniards led by the newly appointed governor of Hispanic Texas arrived in Natchitoches, Louisiana.[1] Governor Manuel María de Salcedo was no stranger on the Louisiana-Texas frontier. At the beginning of the nineteenth century, before Spain ceded Louisiana to France, Salcedo, as an infantry captain, had ably assisted his sick and aged father, Juan Manuel de Salcedo, in administering the province from New Orleans.[2] In fact, the senior Salcedo, the ninth and last governor of Spanish Louisiana, had kept his eldest son so busy with official routine that Don Manuel had hardly had time to answer personal correspondence.[3] For instance, in 1800, when the government of

[1] Dr. John Sibley to Henry Dearborn, Secretary of War, Natchitoches, September 7, 1808, Record Group 107, National Archives, Washington, D.C. Hereinafter cited as NA.

[2] J. Villasana Haggard, "The Counter-Revolution of Béxar, 1811," *Southwestern Historical Quarterly*, 43, no. 2 (October, 1939), 222–223 n.

[3] Salcedo to Pedro Favrot, September 11, 1801; Favrot to Juan Manuel de

Spain agreed to transfer the territory to Napoleon Bonaparte, Salcedo served as a boundary commissioner, a task that undoubtedly required the preparation of detailed reports.[4] By 1808 Don Manuel had acquired sufficient training in colonial administration to qualify him for his new assignment in Texas.

Accompanied by his wife and daughter, a chaplain, and domestic servants, Governor Salcedo tarried for about four days at Natchitoches, a strategic outpost from which the United States government conveniently obtained intelligence on conditions in New Spain. Since the previous May the Salcedo party had leisurely toured the northeastern and trans-Appalachian regions. After disembarking at New Bedford, Massachusetts, they traveled by stagecoach first to Providence and then to New Haven. Changing to water conveyance, the group visited New York and from there boarded a coach for Philadelphia and Pittsburgh. Then they booked passage on a riverboat and cruised down the Ohio and Mississippi rivers as far south as Natchez. Finally the governor and his companions made the overland trip to Natchitoches.[5]

In view of the physical fatigue of his fellow travelers, Salcedo might have extended his stay at the Louisiana outpost. Certainly the accommodations he found there were not of the best quality, but he took advantage of the opportunity of dining and conversing with John Sibley, United States Indian agent, and Colonel Constant Freeman, an officer stationed at Fort Claiborne.[6] It seems highly probable, however, that the new governor of Texas delayed his departure for San Antonio de Béxar long enough to

---

Salcedo, July 26, 1801; *Transcriptions of Manuscript Collections of Louisiana. no. 1. The Favrot Papers, 1799–1801*, pp. 111, 122; Alcée Fourtier, *A History of Louisiana*, II, 221.

[4] William Campbell Binkley, *The Expansionist Movement in Texas, 1826–1850*, p. 6.

[5] Sibley to Dearborn, Natchitoches, September 7, 1808, NA.

[6] *Ibid.*

obtain as much information about Anglo-American interests as
might be useful to him later. To be sure, Salcedo knew that his
generous hosts in Louisiana had much more than a casual concern about what took place in the land beyond the Sabine River.

As a matter of fact, Salcedo made such a positive impression on
the Indian agent that Sibley promptly informed the War Department of the meeting. Sibley described the Texas executive as
being "about 35 years of Age, A modest unassuming man &
appears to have Sense enough to govern Such people As he will
find there [in Texas]."[7]

Civil pleasantry notwithstanding, Salcedo was quite anxious
to arrive at his final destination. Almost as soon as he reached
Natchitoches he wrote to Antonio Cordero, governor of Coahuila
on special assignment in Texas, advising him of his intention to
set out for Béxar within a short time. Moreover, in keeping with
military courtesy, he enclosed a similar message for his uncle,

---

[7] *Ibid.* Actually, Governor Salcedo—whose full name was Manuel María
de la Concepción Josef Agustín Eloy de Salcedo y Quiroga—was thirty-one
years old when the Council of the Indies assigned him to the Texas frontier
on April 24, 1807. Born in Málaga, Spain, on April 3, 1776, to Juan Manuel
de Salcedo and Francisca de Quiroga y Manso, Manuel de Salcedo enrolled at
the early age of seven at the Royal Academy of Ocaña, after which he transferred to the Royal Seminary of Nobles, where he received instruction until
his seventeenth birthday. Later, as an infantry lieutenant, Salcedo served
under his father at Santa Cruz de Tenerife in the Canary Islands. In 1801 the
Salcedos arrived in Spanish Louisiana, where Don Manuel assisted his father
in the administration of the province. In New Orleans, the future governor of
Texas met María Guadalupe Prietto y la Ronde, of Hispanic-French ancestry,
whom he married in 1803. The next year, following the formal cession of
Louisiana to the United States, the Salcedos, including the aged and sickly
Juan Manuel, returned to Spain. At Cádiz, while attending to family matters,
Manuel María de Salcedo learned of his appointment as governor of Spanish
Texas and took a preliminary oath of office on May 1, 1807. Then he and his
immediate family departed for North America (Nettie Lee Benson [ed. and
trans.], "A Governor's Report on Texas in 1809," *Southwestern Historical
Quarterly*, 71, no. 4 [April, 1968], 603–605).

Nemesio Salcedo, commandant general of the Interior Provinces.[8]

Manuel Salcedo's anxiety stemmed from information related to him by an American general in Philadelphia, referring to the plans of a Napoleonic emissary, Octaviano D'Alvimar, to revolutionize northern New Spain. In and around Natchitoches it was common knowledge that one month before Salcedo's arrival D'Alvimar had passed through Louisiana on his way west.[9] But Salcedo was unaware that on August 5, 1808, a Spanish patrol from Nacogdoches had arrested the French agent and dispatched him under guard to San Antonio de Béxar and ultimately to San Juan de Ulúa, the dreaded dungeon in Veracruz harbor.[10] In any event, Governor Salcedo, genuinely worried about the safety of his family, entrusted their care to Sibley and hurriedly departed for Texas.[11]

As Don Manuel traversed the wooded terrain on his way to Nacogdoches, the first stopover on the long trip to the Texas capital, Antonio Cordero managed affairs from the center of the province. Upon receiving Salcedo's letter, Cordero sent a prompt reply in which he congratulated Salcedo on his appointment to the governorship and apprised the Texas executive on conditions in Spain, adding that he would continue his role as caretaker of the government until Don Manuel arrived in Béxar.[12]

[8] Salcedo to Antonio Cordero, Natchitoches, September 8, 1808, Béxar Archives, Eugene C. Barker Texas History Center, The University of Texas at Austin. Hereinafter cited as BA.

[9] Sibley to Dearborn, Natchitoches, September 7, 1808, NA.

[10] Nettie Lee Benson (ed. and trans.), *Report that Dr. Miguel Ramos de Arizpe Priest of Borbon, and Deputy in the Present General and Special Cortes of Spain for the Province of Coahuila One of the Four Eastern Interior Provinces of the Kingdom of Mexico Presents to the August Congress on the Natural, Political and Civil Condition of the Provinces of Coahuila, Nuevo León, Nuevo Santander, and Texas of the Four Eastern Interior Provinces of the Kingdom of Mexico*, p. 17 n. 86. Hereinafter cited as *Arizpe Report*.

[11] Sibley to Dearborn, Natchitoches, September 7, 1808, NA.

[12] Cordero to Salcedo, Béxar, September 12, 1808, BA.

In the meantime, from the commandant general's headquarters in Chihuahua, a courier brought two important communications that altered the political structure in Texas. One dispatch merely contained Salcedo's commission as governor. More significant, however, was the second message, which conferred on Cordero a promotion as deputy to the commandant general in both Coahuila and Texas.[13] In reality, Cordero's assignment meant that he outranked Salcedo.

Unaware of the recent changes that had gone into effect at the capital, Governor Salcedo, upon reaching Nacogdoches in October, informed the *audiencia* of Guadalajara, the judicial court that exercised jurisdiction over Texas, of his arrival in New Spain to take charge of affairs in the province.[14] Shortly thereafter the governor received a request from Cordero to present himself in Béxar at the earliest convenience for the express purpose of taking the oath of office.[15]

Exactly when Don Manuel arrived at the capital cannot be determined, but late in October Cordero sent a report to him in Béxar, discussing a problem that annoyed most Hispanic administrators—the contraband trade at Bayou Pierre in East Texas.[16] By the end of the month the governor was evidently in San Antonio, and perhaps he spent a few days resting from the rigor of the strenuous trip. Quite likely, too, he took up quarters at the executive residence, where he and Cordero no doubt talked about the vital questions affecting the defense of Texas—such as the D'Alvimar incident—as well as personal topics that Hispanics generally feel a natural compulsion to discuss. The two men had a common bond that antedated their service in the Interior

[13] Nemesio Salcedo to Cordero, Chihuahua, September 30, 1808, BA.

[14] Salcedo to Regent of the Royal Audiencia of Guadalajara, Nacogdoches, October 10, 1808, BA.

[15] Cordero to Salcedo, Béxar, October 13, 1808, BA.

[16] Cordero to Salcedo, Béxar, October 25, 1808, BA.

Provinces. Cordero, born of a noble family in Cádiz in 1753, had grown to early manhood in Madrid with three of Don Manuel's uncles, one of whom was the commandant general.[17] This social connection unquestionably influenced Nemesio Salcedo's selection of Cordero as his assistant. Zebulon Pike met with Don Antonio and described him in the following manner:

Cordero is about 5 feet 10 inches in height, 50 years of age, with fair complexion and blue eyes; he wore his hair turned back, and in every part of his deportment was legibly written "the soldier." He yet possessed an excellent constitution, and a body which appeared to be neither impaired by the fatigues of the various campaigns he had made, nor disfigured by the numerous wounds received from the enemies of his king. He was one of the select officers who had been chosen by the court of Madrid to be sent to America about 35 years since, to discipline and organize the Spanish provincials. . . . Through the parts we explored he was universally beloved and respected; and when I pronounce him by far the most popular man in the internal provinces, I risk nothing by the assertion. He spoke the Latin and French languages well, was generous, gallant, brave, and sincerely attached to his king and country. Those numerous qualifications advanced him to the rank of colonel of cavalry . . .[18]

On November 7, 1808, Manuel de Salcedo officially assumed the governorship of Texas. For Cordero the event probably meant a slight relief. Since October, 1805, he had been in Béxar acting as interim executive, but, even though he competently guided affairs through critical times, especially the Neutral Ground crisis,[19] it seems that he really preferred something more

[17] Nettie Lee Benson, "Texas Failure to Send a Deputy to the Spanish Cortes, 1810–1812," *Southwestern Historical Quarterly*, 64, no. 1 (July, 1960), 20–21 n. 21.

[18] Elliott Coues (ed.), *The Expeditions of Zebulon Montgomery Pike, to Headwaters of the Mississippi River, through Louisiana Territory, and in New Spain, during the Years, 1805–6–7*, II, 700.

[19] Carlos E. Castañeda, *Our Catholic Heritage in Texas, 1519–1936*, V, 345–

permanent and rewarding than the task of holding down a post pending the arrival of a duly commissioned successor. So, with Salcedo in control of political questions and routine military matters, Cordero began to devote more attention to his obligations as deputy commandant general. Apparently neither cavalier found any reason why they could not work together in the borderland province.

Governor Salcedo gradually acquainted himself with the various problems of his office. For instance, he processed all military reports submitted to him by subordinate commanders at distant outposts; he prepared instructions concerning the election of municipal officers; he pondered the advisability of permitting Louisiana inhabitants of Hispanic descent to settle in Texas; and he even deliberated the thorny issue of ordering the apprehension of fugitive Negro slaves from the United States.[20]

Whether Salcedo truly believed that he could resolve the question of the runaway slaves is debatable, but the problem occurred at the beginning of his administration, and, as reports from frontier commanders continued to discuss the matter, he dealt with it both within and without the scope of his powers. In January, 1809, the commandant at Trinidad notified Salcedo that some Negroes had fled through the vicinity of his post but that efforts were being made to capture them.[21] Before the month ended, with Salcedo still unable to cope with the East Texas situation, the commandant general insinuated himself into the question. In a letter to the governor of Louisiana, Don Nemesio expressed

350; Benson, "Texas Failure to Send a Deputy to the Spanish Cortes," p. 21 n. 21.

[20] José María Guadiana to Cordero, Nacogdoches, December 4, 1808; Pedro López Prietto to Salcedo, Trinidad, December 6, 1808; Cordero to Salcedo, Béxar, December 15, 1808; Salcedo to Nemesio Salcedo, Béxar, December 15, 1808, BA.

[21] Pedro López Prietto to Salcedo, Trinidad, January 23, 1809, BA.

his willingness to maintain friendly relations with the United States over the disposal of the refugees.[22] This expression, of course, was far from a workable solution, but undoubtedly it removed the possibility of renewed border tensions. Meanwhile Salcedo's subordinate officers, closer to the actual problem, kept their superior periodically informed on what transpired in East Texas. From Nacogdoches Salcedo received a dispatch about the recovery of fugitive slaves by their masters.[23] Another commander, at Villa de Salcedo, reported that some Negroes had supposedly escaped in the direction of La Bahía.[24] Thus the problem remained undecided.

In truth, neither of the Salcedos legally resolved the issue of the runaway slaves. Don Nemesio, despite his expression of willingness to maintain amicable relations with the United States, lacked the diplomatic authority to enter into negotiations. Besides, he refused to seek such emergency power, claiming that the priorities of the Napoleonic war in Europe precluded all other considerations. Governor Salcedo, on the other hand, casually disobeyed his uncle's instructions and extralegally permitted the slave owners to reclaim their property. Ultimately, the problem corrected itself when potential Negro refugees realized that they would not find asylum in Hispanic Texas and stayed out of the province.[25]

Even more delicate than the matter of the runaway slaves was the controversy concerning a group of United States army deserters who sneaked through the piney woods into Nacog-

[22] Nemesio Salcedo to Governor of Louisiana [William C. C. Claiborne], Chihuahua, January 29, 1809, BA.

[23] Commandant [José María Guadiana] to Salcedo, Nacogdoches, February 18, 1809, BA.

[24] Antonio Sáenz to Salcedo, Villa de Salcedo, February 22, 1809, BA.

[25] J. Villasana Haggard, "The Neutral Ground between Louisiana and Texas, 1806–1821," *Louisiana Historical Quarterly*, 28, no. 4 (October, 1945), 1073.

doches. On December 23, 1808, Salcedo reported the incident to
Cordero. The same day, the deputy commandant general instructed the governor to investigate the intentions of the new-
comers. But on the following day, before Salcedo could launch
an investigation, Cordero directed him to have the deserters
brought to Béxar.[26] Resolute as Cordero's decision appeared, the
problem dragged on for months. While other duties took up the
time and attention of Hispanic officials, the six deserters evidently remained in custody in East Texas. In April, 1809, two of
the prisoners escaped, but the alerted commander at Trinidad
succeeded in recapturing them.[27] Obviously, keeping the deserters in detention was an ineffective solution because it required
maintaining constant vigilance over them. Possibly the Spanish
troops on occasion utilized them on public works projects, but,
since this approach presented new opportunities for attempted
escapes, the deserters more than likely remained in custody.

Gradually a practical answer—converting the deserters into
settlers—emerged in the minds of Hispanic authorities. Exactly
who first suggested the idea is unknown, but by May, 1809, the
commandant general gave his qualified support to the plan.
What he particularly wanted was assurance that the deserters
were sincerely interested in becoming settlers and not in engaging in clandestine activities. For this reason, Don Nemesio ordered the transfer of the Anglo-American interlopers to Béxar
for intensive interrogation. Before the directive could be carried
out, however, the senior commander, acting on new advice, re-
versed his decision and instructed Texas officials to close the
frontier to army deserters from the United States.[28]

When Don Nemesio's order reached San Antonio, the only

[26] Salcedo to Cordero, Béxar, December 23, 1808; Cordero to Salcedo, December 23, 24, 1808. BA.
[27] Sáenz to Salcedo, Trinidad, April 8, 10, 1809. BA.
[28] Castañeda, *Our Catholic Heritage in Texas*, V, 392.

official who objected was Governor Salcedo. He declared that arresting Napoleonic spies who posed as prospective settlers was justifiable, but to deny entrance to bona fide colonists from former Hispanic lands was wholly unrealistic. Moreover, Don Manuel realized that it was virtually impossible to police the entire East Texas frontier to prevent violations to Spain's territorial integrity. Therefore the governor proposed the formation of a policy that would make allowances for immigrants who could demonstrate their loyalty. Furthermore, he reinforced his argument by pointing out that an Anglo-American deserter, denied permission to settle, would in desperation either join up with outlaws who frequented the Neutral Ground or stealthily return to Hispanic Texas and seek brotherhood with the Indians. Either alternative constituted a threat to the security of the borderlands. To this argument Don Nemesio turned a deaf ear and chastised his subordinate officials in Texas for having the audacity to submit proposals in the first place.[29]

One subordinate officer who had been in Texas since the border crisis of 1805–1806 and who played a vital role in its settlement was Simón de Herrera. Like Cordero, Herrera, as governor of Nuevo León, a province south of the Rio Grande, was on temporary assignment in Texas, but, because of the necessity of guarding the eastern frontier, for three years he had confined his attention to purely military matters. Zebulon Pike in his journal wrote:

Don Simon de Herrara [*sic*] is about 5 feet 11 inches high, has a sparkling black eye, dark complexion and hair. He was born in the Canary Islands, served in the infantry in France, Spain, and Flanders, and speaks the French language well, with a little of the English. He is engaging in his conversation with his equals; polite and obliging to his inferiors, and in all his actions one of the most gal-

[29] *Ibid.*, pp. 392–393.

lant and accomplished men I ever knew. He possesses a great knowledge of countries and societies, and knows how to employ the genius
of each of his subordinates to advantage. . . . He is now lieutenant-
colonel of infantry, and governor of the kingdom of New Leon. His
seat of government is Mont Elrey [Monterrey]; and probably if
ever a chief is adored by his people, it is Herrera.[30]

By early spring of 1809, Simón de Herrera slowly emerged as an
active participant, along with Salcedo and Cordero, in the administration of Hispanic Texas.

As news of Napoleon's invasion of the Iberian peninsula and
the abdication of the king reached New Spain's northern frontier,[31] still another governor—Brigadier General Bernardo Bonavía of Durango—unexpectedly arrived in Texas to strengthen
colonial defenses.[32] Indeed, never in the entire history of the
province had so many high-ranking officers congregated in one
place. No doubt the presence of a fourth governor made Manuel
Salcedo wonder where he fitted in the burgeoning military-polit-
ical bureaucracy. In fact, he complained to the new governor
that the peculiar administrative arrangement in Texas prevented
him from performing his full duty to the soldiers under his
command and to the province as a whole of which he was
governor.[33]

Bonavía's sojourn in Texas was a prelude to a minor reshuffling
of assignments by the commandant general. Apparently satisfied
with Cordero's work in Texas, Don Nemesio now needed him
back in Coahuila. Bonavía was Cordero's replacement, but, since
the new commander was not fully informed on Texas affairs,
Cordero received instructions to remain at his post until Bonavía

---

[30] Coues (ed.), *Pike*, II, 701.
[31] Sáenz to Salcedo, Villa de Salcedo, May 8, 1809, BA.
[32] Nemesio Salcedo to Salcedo, Chihuahua, March 30, 1809, BA.
[33] Salcedo to Bernardo Bonavía, Béxar, May 2, 1809, BA.

completed his orientation.[34] For his own part, Cordero advised
Bonavía that he was ready to turn over the command to him
right away.[35] Salcedo, evidently anxious to reduce the number
of superior officers in Texas by one, expressed his appreciation to
Cordero for his services and offered his assistance in arranging
for Don Antonio's departure.[36]

On April 19, 1809, two days after his arrival in Béxar, Bonavía held a meeting in which he earnestly requested Salcedo,
Herrera, and Cordero to submit to him written opinions on the
most effective approach for defending and developing the province.[37] Accordingly, the three men, influenced by the harsh realities of frontier duty, promptly prepared and forwarded their
candid reports. Cordero's principal idea was to reinforce strategic
Nacogdoches and its immediate environs with immigrant settlers. As a backup defensive measure, he advocated the formation
of a cavalry unit manned by provincials and sufficiently mobile
for limited operations in critical areas. Herrera, with three years'
experience in East Texas, strongly endorsed Cordero's plan for
safeguarding Nacogdoches and further recommended increasing
the size of the standing army. In order to support with adequate
equipment and supplies the large contingent of troops he envis-
ioned, Herrera called for opening a port at Matagorda Bay near
the settlement of La Bahía. Whatever other measures might be
adopted, he warned, under no circumstances should the East
Texas outposts be abandoned, lest Anglo-Americans interpret
such withdrawal as tantamount to Spanish military unprepared-
ness.[38]

---

[34] Castañeda, *Our Catholic Heritage in Texas*, V, 365–366.
[35] Cordero to Bonavía, Béxar, April 9, 1809, BA.
[36] Salcedo to Cordero, Béxar, April 12, 1809, BA.
[37] Bonavía *et al.*, Béxar, April 19, 1809, BA.
[38] Casteñada, *Our Catholic Heritage in Texas*, V, 368–373.

Governor Salcedo, who had a penchant for expressing his views, submitted a penetrating analysis of conditions in Texas. Possibly he felt honor-bound as chief political leader to prepare such a document, for when his comrades-in-arms returned to their home bases of authority, he would be held strictly accountable for what happened in the province. Then, too, the younger Salcedo may have earnestly desired to prove to his uncle, Don Nemesio, that as governor he fully understood, without assistance from well-meaning outsiders, the complexities of the gubernatorial office. Certainly only Salcedo of Texas had had the courage to differ with the commandant general on the question of United States army deserters, an independent position clearly demonstrating that the Texas governorship was professionally important to him. And so, by giving forthright responses, contrary and annoying as they might have been to superior officers, he frequently manifested his interest in serving the empire honorably. For a cavalier like Don Manuel it was an act of disagreeing without being disagreeable.

In his report to Bonavía, Salcedo, basing his comments on his travels through the United States and his service in Hispanic Louisiana under his father, reviewed the aggressive spirit of Anglo-American frontiersmen. Obviously his impressions in Natchitoches were foremost in his mind. Moreover, he asserted that this invasive tendency daily gaining momentum east of the Sabine River constituted a renewed threat to the Spanish borderlands. To guard against foreign encroachment, however minimal, the governor recommended a repopulation program involving a substantial increment of soldiers and settlers. If properly distributed, the new colonists, according to Salcedo, would complement themselves: the troops would provide protection for the farmers, whose future crops, in turn, would furnish foodstuffs for the army. Therefore it was essential for the implementation of Salcedo's plan that the government adopt a flexible approach to colonization, allowing the local authorities the option of creating new settlements in areas of strategic value.[39]

In principle, the three governors' recommendations coincided with General Bonavía's own views, but he still needed to convince Don Nemesio of their validity. The commandant general, faced with the responsibility of guarding the vast sweep of the northern frontier, had already formulated a policy of retreat and retrenchment for East Texas. Hence Bonavía recognized the inherent difficulty in persuading the elder Salcedo to modify his stringent stand. If Hispanic Texans were to do their duty in the defense of God, king, and empire, then they needed a viable military program that vested ample powers in an officer of high rank for dealing with all emergencies and that granted to local commanders the prerogative of utilizing the human and natural resources within the province. In this context, Bonavía argued, Hispanics in Texas should be allowed the privilege of enjoying the benefits of the Bourbon reforms, particularly in trade and commerce. Establishing a port at Matagorda Bay definitely would strengthen the colonial defensive posture by economic rehabilitation of the area.[40]

Regrettably, Bernardo Bonavía's arguments failed to dislodge Commandant General Salcedo from his obstructionist stance. Instead, Don Nemesio ordered Bonavía to maintain the status quo and to close the frontier to all interlopers from Louisiana, regardless of ethnic background.[41] Apparently Don Manuel's uncle, insulated in faroff Chihuahua, distrusted reforms that might be misunderstood or abused by inhabitants in underdeveloped regions.

In view of this setback, Bonavía summoned his chief advisors

---

[39] *Ibid.*, V, 371–372; Salcedo [to Bonavía], Béxar, May 7, 1809, BA.
[40] Castañeda, *Our Catholic Heritage in Texas*, V, 373–374.
[41] *Ibid.*, V, 376.

to meet with him again at his quarters at mid-morning of June
19. In attendance and acting in their military capacities were
Colonel Cordero, Lieutenant Colonel Salcedo, Lieutenant Colonel
Herrera, and Captain Mariano Varela. At this junta, Bonavía
still contended that economic improvement and adequate defense
were the two edges of the sword, but that without Don Nemesio's
consent this approach, however high-minded, would be stifled.
But Bonavía refused to be thwarted. He understood his superior
officer's strong dislike for innovations that involved sizable expenditures, and this insight explained why he sought the counsel
of his coworkers in frontier Béxar for a pragmatic solution in order to win the commandant general's approval. In essence, Don
Bernardo recommended inviting law-abiding former Spanish
subjects in United States Louisiana to relocate in Texas, improving communications in the province, and opening the lands
around the secularized San Antonio missions for settlement and
development. To these proposals the junta members gave their
endorsement; they even went so far as to suggest methods by
which they might be implemented. Encouraged by the enthu-
siastic response of his colleagues, Bonavía held another meeting
later in the month to discuss the necessity of direct maritime contact between Texas and Veracruz, and particularly of a free-
trade port. Already, Bonavía reminded his fellow officers, reforms
of the Bourbon monarchs of Spain had provided for the establishment of such a public facility. What disturbed him was why
higher authorities in New Spain had not pursued this goal. In
time, Bonavía learned from the commandant general that opening a port on the Texas coast was out of the question; furthermore, Bonavía's superior officer wondered what had prompted
him to believe that vessels would ever be attracted to sail into
Matagorda Bay.[42]

[42] *Ibid.*, V, 377–383.

Nemesio Salcedo was imperious and autocratic in his relations with his subordinate officers in Texas. Zebulon Pike, who had an unsolicited audience with the commandant general in April, 1807, reported that he had "found the general sitting at his desk; he was a middle-sized man, apparently about 55 years of age, with a stern countenance."[43] Sternly or otherwise, since 1802 Don Nemesio had served the empire in the Interior Provinces of New Spain. He began his military career in approximately 1765 as a cadet in the Royal Spanish Guard and then graduated to an infantry regiment of Navarre in which, for thirteen years, he never advanced above the grade of captain. In Spain's colonial wars in North America, however, Nemesio Salcedo distinguished himself sufficiently so that, upon returning to Europe in 1783, he earned a promotion to the rank of lieutenant colonel. Five years later, upon Charles IV's coronation, Don Nemesio obtained a full colonelcy and the command of a regiment. Still later, in 1790, he successfully petitioned for a prestigious assignment in the Crown Infantry Regiment. Subsequently he was transferred to New Spain, where he quickly won the attention of Viceroy Juan Vicente de Guëmeo Pacheco de Padillo, Conde de Revillagigedo. He ultimately received a further promotion to brigadier general and the command of the Interior Provinces.[44] This, then, was the man who from afar guided Hispanic officials in Texas.

Without doubt the cavaliers in Texas were not lacking in plans for safeguarding the province from internal and external threats. The plans, to be effectively translated into actual accomplishments, required money and imaginative direction from above. As Bonavía and his associates realized, Texas was logically the peripheral buffer that needed to be reinforced, but the province as seen from Chihuahua constituted only one sector of defense

---

[43] Coues (ed.), *Pike*, II, 656.
[44] Luis Navarro García, *Las Provincias Internes en el siglo XIX*, pp. 3–4.

in the arc of the northern borderlands. Hispanic defenders in
Texas, as they experienced one rebuff after another, at best
pondered possible courses of action should an emergency arise;
at worst, they operated in a vacuum for the remainder of the
year.[45] A summary prepared by Governor Salcedo elucidates the
incapabilities that plagued Spanish Texas and its guardians in
1809:

The governor [he wrote] is without *asesor, secretario, escrivano,*
without *aranceles* [customs collectors], *instrucciones*, &c., so that he
is compelled to do everything himself. There are in the province two
presidial companies and one other, whose total of 352 men, united
to those [companies] of Nuevo Reino de Leon and Colonia de Santander number 1033, including officers. They are stationed at Nacogdoches, Atascosito . . . Villa de Trinidad, Bahia del Espiritu Santo,
Bexar, and other places, leaving scarcely 250 men disengaged.[46]

Eventually, one administrator—Antonio Cordero—returned
to Coahuila, where he devoted his attention to more local problems,[47] whereas Salcedo, Herrera, and Bonavía remained steadfast in their assignments. Of the three stalwarts, Governor Salcedo enjoyed the comforts of home life on the frontier. Shortly
after he took his oath of office in November, 1808, his family
evidently joined him in Béxar, because Don Manuel received a
report from East Texas that a teamster, carrying certain posses-
sions belonging to Señora Salcedo, had arrived in Atascosito.[48] In
all probability, the pleasure he derived in having his wife, María

---

[45] Odie B. Faulk, *The Last Years of Spanish Texas, 1778–1821*, pp. 98–99.
[46] *A Twentieth Century History of Southwest Texas*, I, 47–48.
[47] Castañeda, *Our Catholic Heritage in Texas*, V, 421–422; Coues (ed.),
Pike, II, 702.
[48] Commander [of Atascosito] to Cordero, Atascosito, November 23, 1808,
BA.

Guadalupe, and their little daughter, Mariquita,[49] in Spanish Texas amply compensated Don Manuel for the strain on his honor, after more than a year in office, caused by the unavoidable necessity of sharing the gubernatorial authority and responsibility.

[49] Frederick C. Chabot (ed.), *Texas in 1811: The Las Casas and Sambrano Revolutions*, p. 146; Samuel Davenport to Salcedo, Nacogdoches, January 23, 1812, BA.

3. SALCEDO'S STEWARDSHIP
ON THE EVE OF
THE MEXICAN REVOLUTION

THE START OF 1810 offered no relief to the pressures felt by colonial defenders of the Spanish borderlands. East Texas in particular became a critical area of attention for Governor Manuel de Salcedo. Early in January he received reports from his subordinate officers on unsettled conditions along the Sabine River salient. Illustrative of the new mood was a communication from the Nacogdoches commander about two individuals, apparently Anglo-Americans, who grazed a sizable herd of horses between the Cadodacho Indian village in Louisiana and the Sabine River.[1] Certainly the value of horses and the extent to which they might be used by a potential enemy so impressed Hispanic officials in Béxar and elsewhere that they

[1] Salcedo to Bonavía, Béxar, January 2, 1810, Béxar Archives, Eugene C. Barker Texas History Center, The University of Texas at Austin. Hereinafter cited as BA.

frequently discussed the problem. Quite possibly a connection existed between the first report and a subsequent one about horses stolen from the Nacogdoches vicinity, because the East Texas commander pledged to recapture them.[2]

Even more threatening to the security of the province were sporadic incursions by foreigners.[3] Maintaining vigilance on the periphery was a constant factor in the minds of responsible leaders, but, as the new year unfolded, perhaps because of severely inclement weather, defense assumed a greater importance. Because the military contingent in Texas remained, with few exceptions, relatively unchanged, this defense problem very likely compelled frontier administrators to reassign troops at various outposts. For instance, Pedro López Prietto, the officer in charge of the Trinity River settlement, advised Salcedo that he had inspected the detachment along the Brazos River to the east. Apparently satisfied with his inspection, the captain indicated to the governor that, barring objections, he planned to relieve the twenty-five men guarding Atascosito, a post located on the Trinity River near the coast, and to dispatch them to the presidio at La Bahía.[4] Apprising the governor of recent actions, Prietto also informed Salcedo that the Trinidad command needed funds in all departments.[5]

When he submitted such a request, the East Texas commander expected Governor Salcedo to improve the financial picture within a reasonable period. Out of Chihuahua, however, came discouraging news from the commandant general: because the treasury was virtually depleted, new sources of revenue would have to be found for supporting the Texas units, particularly the

[2] Salcedo to Bonavía, Béxar, January 2, 1810, BA.

[3] Bonavía to Salcedo, Béxar, January 4, 1810, BA.

[4] Pedro López Prietto to Salcedo, Trinidad, Letter 114, January 6, 1810, BA.

[5] Prietto to Salcedo, Trinidad, Letter 116, January 6, 1810, BA.

Béxar contingent.[6] Left unmentioned this time was the usual declaration that Hispanic Texans would rise in unison to defend the province in the event of aggression.

Commandant General Nemesio Salcedo seldom missed an opportunity to upbraid his nephew for overlooking some aspect of provincial administration. In January, 1810, for example, Don Nemesio reprimanded the governor for permitting interlopers from Louisiana to cross into Texas. To the elder Salcedo this negligence constituted an intolerable breach of security. Without any consideration as to means, he ordered Don Manuel to expel the intruders and to prohibit them from taking livestock beyond the border.[7]

Even before receiving the latest chastisement from Chihuahua, Governor Salcedo was well aware of new tensions in East Texas. Yet, his best intentions notwithstanding, Don Manuel understood his limitations in the matter. The governor's commanders in the Sabine River sector had provided sufficient intelligence reports on even the approximate number of cattle and horses that Anglo-Americans possessed in the Neutral Ground. In this instance, Salcedo expressed his utter frustration to Deputy Commandant General Bonavía at being unable to deal effectively with the situation because of a lack of resources.[8] At the end of the previous year Salcedo had apparently considered using livestock from the Trinity River outpost and its environs in some way to relieve the financial burden on his administration, but even this approach resulted in failure when the officer in charge of the post sent word that the horses and cattle were in too poor a condition to be driven overland to the capital.[9] In fact, the fiscal aspect had become so critical that the same commander admitted that he

[6] Nemesio Salcedo to Bonavía, Chihuahua, January 9, 1810, BA.

[7] Nemesio Salcedo to Salcedo, Chihuahua, January 9, 1810, BA.

[8] Salcedo to Bonavía, Béxar, January 10, 1810, BA.

[9] Prietto to Salcedo, Trinidad, Letter 126, January 12, 1810, BA.

lacked arms, munitions, and horses with which to carry out his responsibilities.[10]

Deplorable as the situation appeared to him, Don Manuel requested the Spanish officer at Nacogdoches to transmit the latest intelligence regarding possible movements from the United States, general conditions along the border, and especially the attitude of the Indian tribes. No doubt as a gesture to stiffen morale, the governor urged his principal officer in East Texas to remind the garrison to be extremely watchful.[11]

Curiously, after being in office more than a year, Salcedo became increasingly concerned with the question of foreign encroachment. To be sure, the shift in his attitude occurred slowly, almost unnoticeably, until it was discernible in his correspondence with his superiors and subordinates. On January 15, 1810, in a letter to Bernardo Bonavía, Governor Salcedo discussed a communiqué he had received from Luis de Onís, a Hispanic diplomat residing at Philadelphia, warning him to guard against the aggressive intentions of Anglo-American frontiersmen toward the borderlands. Salcedo candidly disclosed that, considering the current shortage of men and capital, he seriously doubted the invincibility of Spanish arms should aggression actually occur.[12] This document clearly showed that Salcedo, manifesting a newly found trust in Bonavía's competency as a royal officer, realistically assessed an untenable situation. To a cavalier like Salcedo the question was not one of assuming a negative stance in order to justify inaction. Certainly the positions he had taken earlier vis-à-vis his uncle signified that Don Manuel had definite ideas about his stewardship. Therefore his concern about Spain's defensive posture in East Texas was a legitimate topic to discuss with his superior officer in the capital, who, like himself, was

[10] Prietto to Salcedo, Trinidad, Letter 129, January 12, 1810, BA.
[11] Salcedo to José María de Guadiana, Béxar, January 14, 1810, BA.
[12] Salcedo to Bonavía, Béxar, January 15, 1810, BA.

conversant with the problem. In doing so, perhaps pragmatism entered into Salcedo's calculations, since a request from Bonavía to Don Nemesio for additional personnel stood a better chance of gaining approval than one that originated in the governor's office.

In the meantime, Don Manuel managed to generate mobility among his military forces by shifting parts of commands to different areas and by demanding that reports be carefully prepared to reflect the latest developments.[13] Then, in an effort to alleviate the exasperating financial problem, the governor issued a proclamation to the people, appealing to their sense of loyalty for support for the royal armies that daily guarded the territorial integrity of the empire—in short, he asked the inhabitants for donations for the upkeep of the troops.[14] It is difficult to ascertain whether Salcedo genuinely expected the populace to respond wholeheartedly—or even half-heartedly—to his plea for contributions; the proclamation might have been a stratagem to dramatize a local urgency to the commandant general. In fact, on the same day that he signed the request for donations, Don Manuel wrote a lengthy explanation to his uncle stating the reasons—principally inadequate resources—why he had delayed the execution of an earlier order calling for the immediate expulsion of foreigners from Spanish soil.[15]

Don Manuel, now unusually apprehensive about alien penetrations, very likely agreed in principle with the expulsion decree but differed in the details. On the other hand, it is entirely possible that the governor, realizing that his frame of reference for East Texas affairs rested wholly on his observations in 1808 and on information furnished by his lieutenants, felt obliged before banishing any undesirable to see for himself the actual conditions of the areas from where he regularly received progress

13 Salcedo to Prietto, Béxar, January 19, 1810, BA.
14 Salcedo to the Inhabitants of Texas, Béxar, January 21, 1810, BA.
15 Salcedo to Nemesio Salcedo, Béxar, January 21, 1810. BA.

reports. On January 23, probably as a routine gesture, Salcedo notified a minor official at San Luis Potosí of his intention to begin an inspection tour of the province on February 12.[16]

Sudden as it might have appeared on the surface, Salcedo's decision to inspect the frontier settlements did not originate overnight in 1810. Actually, this was an old topic of discussion, dating back to February of the preceding year, four months after Salcedo had assumed the governorship, when he had received the commandant general's approval for such an undertaking. For several months thereafter news of the projected trip prompted officials in Nacogdoches, Béxar, and Chihuahua to communicate back and forth on the subject. One junior officer in the capital city, whom Salcedo apparently had planned to leave in charge of administrative duties, notified the commandant at Nacogdoches that in the governor's absence the response to all incoming correspondence would be suspended. Indeed, by Hispanic standards of the borderlands, a tour of the province by the political executive was a well-organized operation in which even Don Nemesio cooperated. When arrangements for the inspection seemed almost completed by April, 1809, the commandant general dispatched the proper credentials to his nephew Manuel for making a *visita* in Nacogdoches, the major outpost in East Texas. One month later, Deputy Commandant General Bonavía requested Governor Salcedo to postpone the trip until final instructions arrived from Don Nemesio.[17] As events turned out, however, the commandant general and his lieutenants preoccupied themselves for the remainder of 1809 with other con-

[16] Salcedo to José Ruíz de Aguirre, Béxar, January 23, 1810, BA.

[17] Nemesio Salcedo to [Salcedo], Chihuahua, February 20, 1809; Antonio Cordero to Nemesio Salcedo, Béxar, March 6, 1809; Mariano Varela to Commandant of Nacogdoches, [Guadiana] Béxar, March 15, 1809; Nemesio Salcedo to Salcedo, Chihuahua, April 17, 1809; Bonavía to Salcedo, Béxar, May 9, 1809, BA.

siderations and neglected the inspection tour. Nevertheless, the trip remained important in the minds of Hispanic officials, including Governor Manuel de Salcedo, who in 1810 as in the year before gave the impression of being vitally interested.

From a chronological viewpoint, the inspection tour was a project that required many months to organize. Yet the proposed expedition of 1810 differed fundamentally from the abortive trip of 1809 in terms of the assumptions upon which frontier defenders based their plans. First, in 1809 Governor Salcedo, hardly more than a quarter-year in office, manifested great confidence and initiative, even going so far as to suggest counterproposals for improving the welfare and defense of the province. By 1810, however, Don Manuel, though still retaining much independence of thought and local action, occasionally expressed dissatisfaction at the way the bureaucracy of the commandancy general thwarted his administration. Second, the plans of the 1809 journey commenced when Antonio Cordero, a cavalier who often agreed with Salcedo's perceptions, was deputy commandant general on special assignment to Texas. Salcedo's association with Cordero was for the most part cordial. After all, the two men had effected a smooth transition in office. But when Bernardo Bonavía replaced Don Antonio, although the official relationship did not deteriorate, Governor Salcedo complained that the top-heavy hierarchy tended to neutralize his authority in Texas. Third, in 1809 Don Manuel, confident of the might of Spanish arms, had boldly suggested absorbing bona fide foreign settlers into the provincial population. Within a year his optimism had turned to apprehension, mainly because the commandant general curtailed the sending of sizable troop replacements. Finally, when Don Manuel assumed the governorship he no doubt had expected to receive the respect and support of the commandant general, especially since the incumbent was his father's brother. To what extent nepotism played a role in the selection of the younger Salcedo for the position in Texas cannot be determined, but Nemesio Salcedo certainly showed no preference to his nephew. In fact, it was just the opposite: Don Nemesio commended almost every high-ranking officer in the borderlands except Don Manuel.

As major preparations for the inspection of the province unfolded, Governor Salcedo busied himself with routine problems. For instance, he pondered the feasibility of regrouping human resources for better defense and protection. One specific removal that he had in mind was the relocation of the settlers at Trinidad to the San Marcos River, an outpost situated closer to the provincial capital, but his uncle, although not manifesting opposition to the plan, ordered him not to initiate any moves until the end of the inspection tour.[18] From Béxar, Don Manuel again reminded the commandant general that, although care was being exercised to prevent foreign intrusions, more troops would be required for efficient frontier service.[19] Meanwhile Captain Prietto at Trinidad reported to the governor that he had reassigned a small contingent at Atascosito.[20]

Because of the new urgency Hispanic officials gave to the governor's inspection of the province, the defensive posture of Nacogdoches assumed increased importance. Don Manuel informed Bernardo Bonavía that the Nacogdoches commander had reported on the activities of two foreigners who grazed horses near the international boundary. Bonavía replied that he would study the situation and render a decision.[21] Not content to wait

[18] Nemesio Salcedo to Salcedo, Chihuahua, January 23, 1810, BA.
[19] Salcedo to Nemesio Salcedo, Béxar, January 23, 1810, BA.
[20] Prietto to Salcedo, Trinidad, January 24, 1810, BA.
[21] Salcedo, to Bonavía, Béxar, January 25, 1810; Bonavía to Salcedo, Béxar, January 26, 1810, BA.

for an answer, Governor Salcedo notified Bonavía that he had dispatched a very confidential letter to the East Texas commander about the necessity of having a conference.[22]

Another problem that continued to plague Don Manuel was inadequate finances. On Saturday, January 27, he notified Bonavía that he had sent to all military detachments in Texas requests for voluntary donations for the support of the army.[23] Shortly thereafter, Don Nemesio, a good bureaucrat with a pen, provided instructions on how such a collection should be conducted.[24] Of all the Spanish officers serving in Texas, only Bonavía had any assurance that eventually he would be paid. Considering the acute fiscal situation everywhere, if the information troubled anyone in the king's service, undoubtedly it was Governor Salcedo, who received a communication from Saltillo explaining that funds had been deposited to pay Bonavía's salary.[25]

Critical as the money situation was in the borderlands at the end of the first decade of the nineteenth century, there were some depositories that contained sufficient reserves to meet minimal demands. The problem, therefore, was not so much one of unavailability of currency as one of authorization to make such expenditures. Governor Salcedo, for example, advised José María de Guadiana, the Nacogdoches commander, that a certain amount of money could be withdrawn from the *mesteña* fund,[26] revenue derived from the sale of licenses for hunting and slaughtering wild livestock.[27] On another occasion Salcedo ordered Guadiana to contact Guillermo Barr, a nominally Hispanicized Anglo-American trader who had permission to operate an East

---

[22] Salcedo to Bonavía, Béxar, January 27, 1810, BA.
[23] Salcedo to Bonavía, Béxar, January 27, 1810, BA.
[24] Nemesio Salcedo to Salcedo, Chihuahua, January 31, 1810, BA.
[25] Manuel Royuela to Salcedo, Saltillo, January 31, 1810, BA.
[26] Salcedo to Guadiana, Béxar, February 3, 1810, BA.
[27] Walter Prescott Webb (ed.), *The Handbook of Texas*, II, 254.

Texas trading center, for the purpose of obtaining seventy-five pesos deposited with Barr, in order to pay two soldiers to whom the money was due.[28] Far more involved than this, however, was the governor's concern over the financial stability of the presidial companies assigned to defend the capital. Such an interest became evident when the paymaster of the company of Béxar briefed Salcedo on the fact that Deputy Commandant General Bonavía held in custody a substantial sum of money from the sale of goods confiscated from a contrabandist, Francisco de la Rosa.[29] For reasons not germane to this historical account, at the time of the De la Rosa incident the presidial company of Parras, through administrative oversight, had suffered a loss of nineteen thousand pesos. Hence it was this amount about which Salcedo, on Friday, February 23, wrote to Bonavía, asking for a reimbursement. On the same day, Don Bernardo acknowledged having access to the money but corrected the record by indicating that it had been erroneously discounted against the balance sheets of the companies of Béxar and Parras.[30] Within ten days after the exchange of such correspondence, Salcedo received the nineteen thousand pesos and distributed the amount between the two presidial units.[31]

The transfer of funds, when completed, temporarily improved the financial situation at the capital, but the ultimate responsibility for the welfare of the entire province rested with Governor

[28] Salcedo to Guadiana, Béxar, February 20, 1810, BA. For a detailed account of the trading activities of Barr, see J. Villasana Haggard, "The Houses of Barr and Davenport," *Southwestern Historical Quarterly*, 44, no. 1 (July, 1945), 66–88.

[29] Andrés Benito Courbiere to Salcedo, Béxar, February 22, 1810, BA. For an account of the De la Rosa incident, see Carlos E. Castañeda, *Our Catholic Heritage in Texas: 1519–1936*, V, 353–356.

[30] Salcedo to Bonavía, Béxar, February 23, 1810; Bonavía to Salcedo, Béxar, February 23, 1810, BA.

[31] Salcedo to Bonavía, Béxar, March 4, 1810, BA.

Salcedo. To this end he persisted in seeking ways to bolster an untenable position. Fully cognizant that Commandant General Nemesio Salcedo disapproved of his writing about deplorable circumstances in Texas to Luis de Onís in the United States, Don Manuel attempted to vindicate himself to Bernardo Bonavía by explaining that in the current emergency all sources of potential aid should be contacted. In fact, to make the matter somewhat palatable to Don Nemesio, Governor Salcedo urged Bonavía to countersign the communications to Onís.[32] To his uncle, Don Manuel reported that, although he had received the letter in which the commandant general reprimanded him for not expelling all foreigners in Texas, he had purposely delayed carrying out the directive until he had properly assessed the latest intelligence from Onís about the activities of aggressive Anglo-American frontiersmen east of the Sabine River. Pending the outcome of that assessment, in the light of new developments, the governor had no choice but to wait for further instructions from Chihuahua.[33]

In the interim Hispanic officials in Texas turned once more to resolving last-minute details concerning Governor Salcedo's inspection of the province. Bernardo Bonavía prepared a set of instructions covering the examination of roads, river crossings, water level of streams, army outposts, and the movements and friendliness or hostility of Indian tribes. Obviously the thoroughness that the deputy commandant general expected the governor to give to the task called for meticulous exactitude, a criterion of which Salcedo was well aware.[34] Early in March, Don Manuel notified his uncle that, due to the paymaster's illness, he had postponed the start of the tour, but he assured the commandant

[32] Salcedo to Bonavía, Béxar, February 26, 1810, BA.

[33] Salcedo to Nemesio Salcedo, Béxar, March 1 [?], 1810, BA.

[34] Bonavía to Salcedo, Béxar, March 1, 1810; Salcedo to Bonavía, Béxar, March 2, 1810, BA.

general that as soon as the *habilitado* recovered, possibly in three or four days, the trip would get underway.[35]

While the governor waited for the paymaster to regain his health, he reviewed dispatches from East Texas, particularly Nacogdoches, and kept his superiors informed on his administrative endeavors. One bit of news from José María de Guadiana, which showed the uneasiness that gripped Hispanic defenders, referred to an issue of a United States newspaper that had been sent directly to Don Nemesio in Chihuahua for his appraisal. In his zeal to demonstrate how carefully he guarded the eastern frontier, Guadiana unwittingly gave the commandant general another item with which to worry Texas officials. To expedite the paper work once the inspection tour began, Salcedo transmitted to Guadiana a copy of Spanish law on mortgages, the contents of which he wanted known by all military officers along the Sabine River salient, including Trinidad. Moreover, to coordinate more effectively the mail service between the capital and East Texas, especially in view of the planned trip, the governor ordered a new change in the schedule.[36] In distant Monclova, Antonio Cordero, the Texas governor's former associate, reassured Salcedo that in the event of Anglo-American aggression royalist forces in Coahuila were prepared to lend support to Texas' defenses.[37] How much credence Salcedo placed in this promise is unknown, but possibly it lifted his morale.

Presently, the commandant general sent to Don Manuel the latest instructions pertaining to the inspection journey. In addition to the usual warnings about vigilance, he ordered the Texas executive not to proceed beyond Nacogdoches.[38] In the interval,

---

[35] Salcedo to Nemesio Salcedo, Béxar, March 2, 1810, BA.

[36] Guadiana to Salcedo, Nacogdoches, March 14, 1810; Salcedo to Guadiana, Béxar, March 4, 5, 1810, BA.

[37] Cordero to Salcedo, Monclova, March 6, 1810, BA.

[38] Nemesio Salcedo to Salcedo, Chihuahua, March 6, 1810, BA.

on Friday, March 9, Salcedo advised a leading member of the
town council in Béxar that, barring unforeseen hindrances, he
anticipated leaving the following Sunday. Exercising his gubernatorial prerogative, he appointed Captain Mariano Varela, with
the temporary rank of lieutenant governor, as head of the presidial troops and of the political department at the capital.[39]

We can conjecture that, on Sunday, March 11, perhaps after
hearing mass in the church adjacent to the presidio, Governor
Salcedo said farewell to his wife and daughter, then to Bernardo
Bonavía and the *cabildo* members, and last to the *vecinos*
(urban landowners) who assembled on the main plaza to
see him lead the caravan out of Béxar. The personnel who accompanied him very likely included a standard-bearer, a troop
of cavalry with supply wagons, a unit of foot soldiers, a few
personal attendants, and the paymaster. As the entourage slowly
made its way through the rugged streets, crossed the irrigation
ditch, and finally forded the San Antonio River, beyond which
stretched the Camino Real, Don Manuel doubtlessly recounted
in his mind the vicissitudes of his administration. Certainly the
discomfort of having to satisfy the whims of two superiors had
strained his patience, and now the inspection tour offered something of a release.

As the governor's party traversed the royal road to East Texas,
a courier eventually overtook them and delivered supplementary
instructions from Don Nemesio. The commandant general, dis-
carding the obstinacy that characterized his decrees, now ordered
Don Manuel to use discretion in expelling foreigners from
Spanish territory. To be sure, Don Nemesio included references
to previous directives for maintaining security on the frontier,
but the new note embraced in principle all that Governor Salcedo
had urged in the past about dealing with the problems of alien

[39] Salcedo to Luis Galán, Béxar, March 9, 1810, BA.

encroachment. Essentially, the commandant general called for gradual and selective expulsion instead of total and immediate dismissal.[40] Specifically, Don Nemesio instructed his nephew to act firmly but fairly in dealing with immigrants who had illegally entered Texas. To those who indicated a desire to leave the province immediately, the commandant general directed the governor to grant safe passage to the border; others who felt that the case should be reviewed were to be informed that the matter would be processed through proper channels. Under no circumstances, however, was Don Manuel to allow settlers to relocate in the interior to the west.[41]

It seems highly probable that Don Manuel's earlier assessments, coupled with the intelligence reports from East Texas commanders and Luis de Onís about clandestine activities in Louisiana, convinced the elder Salcedo of the necessity of modifying his rigid policy concerning immigrants. Another factor that may have influenced Don Nemesio's thinking was uncertainty about how a high-ranking representative on the periphery of the Spanish empire might react if confronted by armed resistance. Governor Salcedo was flexible in his approach to internal administration; still, he was a proud servant of the king's interests in Texas, and how he would defend this honor was an imponderable factor to Don Nemesio. Obviously the last thing the commandant general needed was the precipitation of a border incident.

On Saturday, March 24, the Texas governor and his party arrived at a small outpost on the east bank of the Trinity River, established by Antonio Cordero in 1805 as Santísima Trinidad de Salcedo. Evidently the trip from the capital to Villa de Salcedo had exhausted Don Manuel, because he manifested no great interest in ferreting out undesirable aliens. Instead, he merely examined census reports and held conferences with the local pastor,

[40] Nemesio Salcedo to Salcedo, Chihuahua, March 13, 1810, BA.
[41] Castañeda, *Our Catholic Heritage in Texas*, V, 424.

Father José Francisco Maynes, who staunchly defended the deportment of his communicants, as well as the conduct of the few foreigners who lived in the vicinity. The governor accepted at face value everything the padre related to him and dispatched a report to his uncle assuring him of the settlers' lawfulness and apparent loyalty. Don Manuel included one significant exception, however: that educated Anglo-Americans—principally traders, lawyers, and physicians—and Frenchmen were the type of trespassers who usually instigated border disturbances.[42]

While Manuel de Salcedo inspected East Texas, observing the realities of frontier defense, an important change of policy occurred. Since the time when he had assumed the commandancy general of the Interior Provinces, Don Nemesio had pursued a hard line toward foreign encroachment, especially along the Sabine River boundary and its proximity to the Neutral Ground, where lawless bands congregated without fear of punishment. That he showed signs of relaxing his intransigency in 1810 became evident in the supplementary instructions to the Texas governor. Presumedly, Salcedo's steadfast convictions ultimately persuaded the commandant general to delegate discretionary powers to Hispanic Texas administrators in dealing with local problems. The policy change meant that Bonavía possessed authority, shared to a lesser degree by Salcedo, to determine the legitimacy of lands occupied by alien settlers.[43] In the wake of their newly won concession, frontier defenders hardly considered the possibility that Don Nemesio frequently reserved the prerogative to reverse his decisions. For the time being, however, he tempered obstinacy with prudence.

Upon completing his work at the Trinity River settlement, Governor Salcedo hurried to Nacogdoches, the most critical outpost in East Texas, where he immediately inspected the fort and the

42 *Ibid.*, V, 309, 424–426.
43 *Ibid.*, V, 426–427.

troops assigned to it.[44] If Don Manuel felt dismay, he kept his own counsel. To be sure, the deterioration of Spain's military strength in Texas was one topic that he repeatedly discussed with his colleagues and superiors. In this context, it is even conceivable that he sensed the futility of staging a show of force in the event of aggression. On the other hand, cavalier that he was, Governor Salcedo hopefully expected the situation to improve. Obviously, in his way of thinking, his presence on the borderland signified the essence of Spain's imperial might, apart from internal stresses and strains, to foreigners with hostile intentions.

The low level of military preparedness notwithstanding, Governor Salcedo's visit to Nacogdoches prompted army personnel in East Texas to display unusual vigor. Clearly the Hispanics, as evidenced by their actions, made a sharp distinction between alien settlers who engaged in peaceful pursuits of the soil and chronic trespassers who entered for illicit purposes. The commander at Atascosito, the outpost located downstream from the villa on the Trinity, promised Don Manuel that he would alert his men to be watchful for potential aggressors emanating from New Orleans, especially in view of current rumors about a revolt being planned by discontented Spaniards in league with Frenchmen and Anglo-Americans.[45] So widespread were these rumors that when Salcedo stopped at Trinidad, even before he arrived in the piney woods, the Nacogdoches officer sent out a detachment of troops to patrol the Sabine River watershed.[46] Subsequently the Texas executive, apparently concerned about the immunity from arrest enjoyed by lawless elements in the Neutral Ground, seized the initiative by suggesting to John C. Carr, justice of the peace at Natchitoches, the necessity of dispatching armed expeditions —twelve Hispanics matched by an equal number of Anglo-

[44] *Ibid.*
[45] José Antonio Aguilar to Salcedo, Atascosito, April 1, 1810, BA.
[46] Salcedo to Bonavía, Trinidad, April 7, 1810, BA.

Americans—into the zone between the Sabine River and the Arroyo Hondo.[47] Judge Carr showed interest in the proposal, but he quickly dissociated himself from any responsibility by referring the matter to the governor of Louisiana. One high-ranking United States Army officer at Fort Claiborne, very likely anticipating international complications, objected to Salcedo's suggestion for sending Hispanic soldiers into the Neutral Ground, but, unable to prevent such action completely, he asked the Texas governor to defer the decision.[48] Although nothing constructive resulted immediately from this interchange of letters, the communication exemplified Governor Salcedo's propensity, when left on his own initiative, for confronting a problem that directly affected his stewardship. For Hispanic Texas officials, the prospect of sending a detachment across the border undoubtedly reinforced the assumption that mobility, albeit limited, was preferable to inaction.

Certainly by 1810 the presence of outlaws in the Neutral Ground was an issue that frontier officials on both sides of the Sabine generally agreed had to be worked out with minimal friction. Yet, since the search for a workable method required diplomatic finesse, army commanders of the two nations shared the credit and the blame for delaying an expeditious settlement. Salcedo advised Bonavía that the Nacogdoches scouting parties sent to the Sabine had not accomplished anything, but he pledged that arrests would be made when Spanish and Anglo-American detachments invaded the Neutral Zone.[49] Sluggishly as the Hispanic bureaucratic wheels seemed to turn, the representatives of Anglo-American officialdom in Natchitoches were equally dila-

[47] Bonavía to Salcedo, Béxar, April 8, 1810; Salcedo to Juan C. Carr, Nacogdoches, April 13, 1810, BA.

[48] Carr to Salcedo, Natchitoches, April 16, 1810; G. Wolfstonecraft [Wollstonecraft] to Salcedo, Natchitoches, April 16, 1810, BA.

[49] Salcedo to Bonavía, Nacogdoches, April 18, 1810, BA.

tory. Judge Carr advised Bonavía that the Louisiana governor had gone to Washington, D.C., to confer with the president of the United States regarding specific action on the Neutral Ground question.[50] In turn, the deputy commandant general opined to Salcedo that Anglo-American leaders, when pressed for quick responses to crucial problems, employed clever stratagems to delay executing an unpleasant task.[51] After considerable deferment, the American general at Fort Claiborne, near Natchitoches, notified Don Manuel that the Madison administration had granted authorization for the United States Army in Louisiana to cooperate with Hispanic officials in expelling intruders from the Neutral Ground. By this time—midsummer of 1810—even Judge Carr was eager to lend his support.[52] For the remainder of the summer, beyond the conclusion of Governor Salcedo's inspection, messengers continually crossed the border. At the easternmost outpost, the Nacogdoches commander, on whose shoulders rested responsibility for the security of East Texas, dutifully informed Salcedo whenever dispatches arrived from foreign soil.[53] Ultimately Bonavía decided on a course of action. During the second week of July, in concert with Manuel de Salcedo, the deputy commandant general replied to the American army officer at Natchitoches that on Wednesday, August 1, Hispanic soldiers—in unison with United States troops, he hoped—would invade the Neutral Ground for the purpose of dislodging lawless intruders.[54]

Forthwith Governor Salcedo directed Guadiana, the Nacogdoches commandant, to prepare for joint action with United

[50] Carr to [Bonavía], Natchitoches, May 23, 1810, BA.

[51] Bonavía to Salcedo, Béxar, June 6, 1810, BA.

[52] Wollstonecraft to Salcedo, Fort Claiborne, July 7, 1810; Carr to Bonavía, Natchitoches, July 8, 1810, BA.

[53] Guadiana to Salcedo, Nacogdoches, July 11, 1810, BA.

[54] Bonavía to Salcedo, Béxar, July 17, 1810, BA.

States troops.[55] All the while the East Texas garrison tensed. Guadiana reported to his superiors in Béxar that he had heard rumors that the Anglo-American authorities in Natchitoches had ordered settlers in the Neutral Ground to evacuate their homes in anticipation of an impending invasion. Salcedo, in advising Bonavía of the latest intelligence, complained that little faith could be placed in the word of the United States Army officer in Natchitoches.[56] Be that as it may, Hispanic officials in Texas remained firm in their determination to clear the Neutral Zone of undesirable elements.

In Nacogdoches, Guadiana arranged for his expedition east of the Sabine River. He notified the Texas governor of his plans to leave the presidio on Sunday, July 29. In his absence, the command of the outpost devolved on Gregorio Amador.[57] As ordered, the Nacogdoches commandant proceeded eastward with a contingent of fifteen men to keep his rendezvous with the Anglo-American forces on August 1. For approximately two weeks the combined units patrolled the Neutral Zone, expelling intruders and destroying their habitats so as to discourage reentry when the soldiers had completed their assignment.[58] In the summer of 1810 there was no way of determining the effectiveness of the expulsion, but in terms of short-range objectives the expedition was a success. In fact, Bonavía, through Salcedo, extended his commendation to Guadiana.[59] Moreover, Don Bernardo unhesitatingly instructed the Texas governor to deduct the expenses for the expedition and consequent expulsions from the *mesteña*

[55] Salcedo to Guadiana, Béxar, July 17, 1810, BA.

[56] Guadiana to Salcedo, Nacogdoches, July 19, 1810; Salcedo to Bonavía, Béxar, July 25, 1810, BA.

[57] Guadiana to Salcedo, Nacogdoches, July 27, 1810; Gregorio Amador to Salcedo, Nacogdoches, July 30, 1810, BA.

[58] Castañeda, *Our Catholic Heritage in Texas*, V, 396; Guadiana to Salcedo, Neutral Zone, July 29–August 15, 1810, BA.

[59] Bonavía to Salcedo, Béxar, August 24, 1810, BA.

fund.[60] In terms of long-range effects, the invaders failed to achieve the objective of permanently clearing the Neutral Ground of obnoxious bands,[61] but the manner in which both contingents handled the issue reflected restraint and resolve.

While the preceding events took place, Governor Salcedo, newly arrived in Nacogdoches, reviewed nonmilitary problems, one of which concerned the immigrants and the lands they occupied. Don Manuel reported to his uncle that the settlers lacked documents and deeds to support their land claims.[62] Despite the handicaps he endured, particularly with reference to inadequate administrative personnel, Governor Salcedo managed remarkably well. According to one source, he partly rectified the situation by issuing "titles to plots of ground, pieces of land, fields, small farms, and large ranches." Perhaps he might have accomplished considerably more had not excessive rains obstructed his movements. He complained to Don Nemesio that in Nacogdoches it rained "more in the secretary's office than . . . outside."[63] In time, the commandant general approved his nephew's conduct of affairs in East Texas, but he cautioned that the land deeds should be issued on a temporary basis.[64]

Inclement weather, the urgency that Hispanic officials ascribed to the mutual invasion of the Neutral Zone, and the usual bureaucratic tardiness may explain why Governor Salcedo glossed over the immigrant aspect of his inspection. Convinced that expulsion for its own sake was negative, the governor quite likely tended to become more lenient when he saw the plight of frontier settlers. To his way of thinking, tillers of the soil, as well as

[60] Bonavía to Salcedo, Béxar, August 31, 1810, BA.

[61] Castañeda, *Our Catholic Heritage in Texas*, V, 396.

[62] Salcedo to Nemesio Salcedo, Nacogdoches, April 18, 1810, BA.

[63] Virginia H. Taylor Houston, "Surveying in Texas," *Southwestern Historical Quarterly*, 45, no. 2 (October, 1961), 207–208; Salcedo to Nemesio Salcedo, Nacogdoches, May 19, 1810, BA.

[64] Nemesio Salcedo to Salcedo, Chihuahua, May 29, 1810, BA.

those involved in other productive pursuits, generally respected law and order. Accordingly, the governor requested the Nacogdoches commander to furnish a list of foreign settlers, indicating occupation, age, place of birth, religious affiliation, and length of residence under Spanish sovereignty. From this report—containing the names of twenty-nine families of the immediate vicinity out of an aggregate population exceeding six hundred souls —Governor Salcedo interrogated the family heads and satisfied himself of their loyalty and worth to the province. Not included in the tour of inspection were the settlements of Bayou Pierre and Atascosito, both of which had alien inhabitants.[65]

That exception seemed significant in light of the uncertainty that gripped East Texas in 1810. Don Manuel worried more about settlers who had fled the province than he did about recent transients, though he undoubtedly realized the potential danger in permitting people of dubious loyalty to remain unchecked. Not surprisingly, he ordered his commanders to arrest foreign interlopers and to transport them to Béxar.[66] The vigilant officer at Trinidad faithfully executed the governor's directive. Even Salcedo himself apprehended a chronic trespasser and, after a hearing, jailed him![67] Ironically, the governor's prisoner was one intruder whom Deputy Commandant General Bonavía, when advised of the capture, expelled from the province with a warning not to return.[68] Apart from these apprehensions, which represented corrective measures, Don Manuel recommended to Bonavía a more effective patrol of the Camino Real by establishing a chain of small outposts from Nacogdoches to San Marcos. Bonavía, aware of deficiencies of personnel and matériel, approved

[65] Castañeda, Our Catholic Heritage in Texas, V, 427, 430–431.

[66] Salcedo to Bonavía, Nacogdoches, April 22, 1810, BA.

[67] Prietto to Salcedo, Trinidad, May 1, 1810; Salcedo to Bonavía, Nacogdoches, May 1, 1810, BA.

[68] Bonavía to Salcedo, Béxar, May 8, 1810, BA.

the deployment of detachments at only two points—at the Colorado River crossing and along the lower road from Trinidad to La Bahía.[69]

In preparation for returning to his office at Béxar, Governor Salcedo reported to a tax collector at San Luis Potosí, probably with the hope of casting an oblique impression on Don Nemesio, that he had assigned all available forces along the border to curtail communication between Hispanic Texans and United States inhabitants.[70] Throughout most of April and May, the governor sent patrols to the Sabine River in a fruitless campaign to search for a French vessel about which friendly Indians related they had been told by other natives. To be sure, the alleged sighting of a foreign ship excited the minds and strained the nerves of Spanish officers from Nacogdoches to Chihuahua.[71] Certainly Don Manuel's soldiers made up in mobility what they lacked in numbers.

The governor's close-up appraisal of fluctuating border conditions prompted him to reiterate to his subordinate officers the grave necessity of maintaining, as best as possible, tight security. He urged them particularly to halt people or correspondence moving in either direction.[72] Even the nominally Hispanicized merchants at Nacogdoches, Guillermo Barr and Samuel Davenport, fell within Don Manuel's purview. From them he requested and obtained cooperation in controlling the flow of unsolicited

[69] Salcedo to Bonavía, Nacogdoches, May 4, 1810; Bonavía to [Salcedo], Béxar, May 8, 1810, BA.

[70] Salcedo to the Intendent of San Luis de Potosí, Nacogdoches, May 17, 1810, BA.

[71] Aguilar to Salcedo, Atascosito, April 17, 1810; Bonavía to Salcedo, Béxar, April 18, 28, 1810; Salcedo to Bonavía, Nacogdoches, May 1, 1810; Bonavía to Nemesio Salcedo, Béxar, May 2, 1810; Bonavía to Salcedo, Béxar, May 8, 1810; Nemesio Salcedo to Bonavía, Chihuahua, May 14, June 12, 1810, BA.

[72] Salcedo to Commanders of Nacogdoches, Trinidad, and Atascosito, Nacogdoches, May 21, 1810, BA.

mail from the United States.[73] Shortly thereafter, as a manifestation of his willingness to do his duty, Davenport delivered a bundle of letters and newspapers to Salcedo, a gesture that ultimately pleased the deputy commandant general because, in his opinion, Anglo-American writers made no secret of their aggressive intentions.[74]

Clearly Hispanic defenders in East Texas subdued papers more effectively than people. The arrival in Nacogdoches of a sergeant and two privates, all deserters from the United States Army, caused them renewed anxiety. Salcedo immediately asked Bonavía for specific instructions on how to cope with the situation.[75] In the interim the governor, assisted by the *cabildo* clerks, interrogated the uninvited intruders; then the Nacogdoches commander lodged the Anglo-Americans in the presidial dungeon.[76] While waiting for further developments, Don Manuel wrote to Bonavía that heavy rains had confined him to his quarters. More importantly, he requisitioned additional personnel and supplies with which to carry out proper service.[77] Possibly the excessive rainfall that restricted the governor's movements also precluded others, even interlopers, from traveling. A week later Don Manuel notified his uncle of the inclement weather that continued to plague East Texas.[78]

Meanwhile, at Béxar, Deputy Commandant General Bonavía and Lieutenant Governor Mariano Varela changed some of the

[73] Salcedo to Commander of Nacogdoches [Guadiana], Nacogdoches, May 21, 1810; William Barr and Samuel Davenport to Salcedo, Nacogdoches, May 22, 1810, BA.

[74] Salcedo to Bonavía, Nacogdoches, May 27, 1810; Bonavía to Commandant General [Nemesio Salcedo], Béxar, June 13, 1810, BA.

[75] Salcedo to Bonavía, Nacogdoches, May 22, 1810, BA.

[76] Salcedo to Commander of Nacogdoches [Guadiana], Nacogdoches, May 22, 1810, BA.

[77] Salcedo to Bonavía, Nacogdoches, May 23, 1810, BA.

[78] Salcedo to Nemesio Salcedo, Nacogdoches, May 29, 1810, BA.

key commanders in the province. They relieved José Agabo de Ayala of the command at La Bahía and in his place assigned Andrés Mateos.[79] Next they transferred the former Bahía commandant to Trinidad to replace Pedro López Prietto, whom they recalled to the capital.[80] Then Don Nemesio sent an unexpected order to Bonavía that affected Varela's status in Texas. Specifically, the governor's uncle advised Don Bernardo that, due to the inability of the lieutenant in charge of Presidio del Rio Grande, he needed Captain Varela to assume command of that post.[81] Even Antonio Cordero, one-time administrator in Spanish Texas, requested Bonavía to expedite the reassignment.[82] Probably because of Governor Salcedo's absence from the capital, and particularly because Don Manuel had left Varela in control of the political office, Bonavía delayed complying immediately with the superior order. On Saturday, June 9, he thanked Don Mariano for his services to the provincial government and informed him of the pending transfer but indicated that it would not take effect until the governor returned from East Texas.[83]

In Nacogdoches Governor Salcedo, preoccupied with the sundry aspects of his inspection, still had the problem of the United States army deserters on his hands. Bonavía undoubtedly expected Don Manuel to resolve the issue without assistance from elsewhere; he wrote to the governor that previous instructions regarding fugitives were applicable—no admittance to anyone.[84] Two days later the deputy commandant general, in apprising Salcedo of the military reassignment at Trinidad, ordered the

[79] Varela to Bonavía, Béxar, May 24, 1810, BA.

[80] Bonavía to Simón de Herrera, Béxar, June 2, 1810; Bonavía to José Agabo de Ayala, Béxar, June 2, 1810, BA.

[81] Nemesio Salcedo to Bonavía, Chihuahua, May 29, 1810, BA.

[82] Cordero to Bonavía, Monclova, June 2, 1810, BA.

[83] Varela to Bonavía, Béxar, June 14, 1810, BA.

[84] Bonavía to Salcedo, Béxar, June 4, 1810, BA.

governor to arrest the three captives.[85] Bonavía's new directive, of course, in no way approached a final solution to the question, and keeping the deserters locked in jail definitely incurred expenses that had to be met. The defense of East Texas improved financially with the delivery of 6,562 pesos to the presidio commander.[86] But, although this amount shored up the presidial treasury, most of the money very likely went to pay overdue salaries. What East Texas needed was massive support, and this was sorely lacking.

By approximately the first week in June, Governor Salcedo, after a three-month tour of inspection, completed preparations for his return trip and left Nacogdoches. To avoid the discomfort of mid-day summer heat, his entourage traveled during the cool mornings and tepid afternoons, a process that resulted in delay, but even then the trip to Béxar doubtlessly took up less time than the eastward journey of the previous spring. On Saturday, June 23, they entered the provincial capital amid the greetings of relatives, neighbors, and soldiers.[87]

While Manuel de Salcedo was homeward bound, Hispanic society in Béxar reassessed its system of values. Knowledgeable members of the ruling gentry recognized that Spain, fountainhead of the civilization to which they belonged, was in the throes of resisting an invasion of French armies. Unquestionably the European crisis shook the empire from its center to the periphery. Spanish Texans, poised on the rim of the borderlands, surely pondered how the emergency would alter their lives. Long-time residents of Béxar no doubt recalled the capture in 1808 of a Napoleonic agent who had haughtily penetrated the eastern border of the province.[88] Since then the commandant

[85] Bonavía to Salcedo, Béxar, June 6, 1810, BA.
[86] Guadiana to Salcedo, Nacogdoches, June 10, 1810, BA.
[87] Diary of Ysidro de la Garza, Béxar, June 23, 1810, BA.
[88] Nettie Lee Benson (ed.), *Report that Dr. Miguel Ramos de Arizpe Priest*

general had warned his fellow officers in Texas that Napoleon, having overturned the royal structure in Spain, threatened the territorial integrity of the empire in North America. He repeatedly cautioned them to guard the frontiers of the Interior Provinces. Moreover, Don Nemesio assured Hispanics in Texas that the mother country, whatever political transitions had taken place in the Iberian peninsula, still functioned through the inauguration of a regency that temporarily governed.[89] At this juncture, Béxar inhabitants of high birth as well as of humble origin needed to reaffirm their faith in the values of their culture.

Accordingly, on Saturday, June 23, the day of Salcedo's anticipated arrival in the capital, Lieutenant Governor Varela summoned royal officers and clergymen to assemble the next day at Bernardo Bonavía's residence for the purpose of pledging their loyalty to the Spanish monarch, Ferdinand VII.[90] As scheduled, the ritual, symbolizing the compact union of church and state, involved every representative who championed the cause of Spain in her moment of urgency. The sword-bearers and the cross-carriers, in their oath of fidelity, presented a harmonious front, signifying to capital dwellers that the core of Hispanic Texas remained firm in its commitment to God and king.[91]

On the same day Bernardo Bonavía dispatched an urgent request to Nemesio Salcedo asking for a clarification of his powers as deputy commandant general, so that he might carry out his

---

of Borbon, and Deputy in the Present General and Special Cortes of Spain for the Province of Coahuila One of the Four Eastern Interior Provinces of the Kingdom of Mexico Presents to the August Congress on the Natural, Political, and Civil Condition of the Provinces of Coahuila, Nuevo León, Nuevo Santander, and Texas of the Four Eastern Interior Provinces of the Kingdom of Mexico, p. 17 n.

[89] Nemesio Salcedo to Salcedo, Chihuahua, May 28, 1810, BA.

[90] Varela to Officers and Clergy, Béxar, June 23, 1810, BA.

[91] Salcedo to Commandant General [Nemesio Salcedo], Béxar, June 27, 1810, BA.

duties more effectively in Hispanic Texas.[92] Most likely the fact
that he had been on special assignment in Texas for more than a
year motivated Bonavía to write for an elaboration of his authority, but Salcedo's homecoming may also have influenced
Don Bernardo's calculations. In any event, the following
Wednesday the two stalwarts became involved in a difference of
opinion when the members of the municipal council elected the
governor as Texas' representative to the newly formed Cortes in
Spain.[93]

Essentially, the election was a response to an edict issued by
the Central Junta of Seville and published in the *Gaceta de
México* on April 15, 1809, which invited Hispanic colonists over-
seas, as citizens of integral components of the empire, to send
representatives to "the governing junta of the kingdom." On
May 28, 1810, Commandant General Salcedo forwarded printed
copies of the decree to his subordinates in the Interior Provinces
and directed them to conduct the elections. When the messages
arrived in Béxar, Manuel de Salcedo was in East Texas; Bernardo Bonavía delayed their execution, reasoning that Texas, besides lacking sufficient population, did not have a nonmilitary
man worthy of the honor. He did concede to Don Nemesio that
the subject of politics was outside his jurisdiction, but nevertheless he declared that selecting an army officer would not necessi-
tate finding resources to pay the delegate's salary. After the
town council's decision of June 27, 1810, Bonavía not surprisingly objected to Salcedo's election on the grounds that Don
Manuel's royal commission as governor disqualified him from
accepting an assignment away from Texas. Just as a direct confrontation between two strong-willed men appeared imminent,
Governor Salcedo disarmed a tense situation by citing a tech-

[92] Bonavía to Commandant General [Nemesio Salcedo], Béxar, June 24,
1810, BA.

[93] Luis Galán *et al.* to Bonavía, Béxar, June 27, 1810, BA.

nicality that in his judgment nullified his election. Since San Fernando de Béxar—or San Antonio de Béxar, the name preferred by local inhabitants—did not have a formal *cabildo*, a prerequisite for the balloting, Don Manuel on June 28 summoned the leading citizens of the capital to solicit their views on the question. Displaying uncommon diplomatic tact, the governor heard the opinions of the *vecinos* and then, without rescinding their decision of the day before, reminded them of his primary obligations as Texas executive, which required him to remain at his post. In reporting the meeting to his uncle, Salcedo wholeheartedly endorsed the selection of Antonio Cordero as dual representative of Texas and Coahuila. Certainly, as far as the political structure of Béxar was concerned, Don Manuel's performance simultaneously secured the respect of capital Hispanics who had voted for him, retained Bonavía's confidence and friendship, and gained valuable time until a higher echelon decided the issue. Ultimately, the *audiencia* of Guadalajara, the court that exercised judicial control over Texas, negated the action of the Béxar council. In fact, because of constant delays, Hispanic Texans lost the opportunity to elect a deputy to the Cortes in Spain.[94]

Having preserved unity among the gentry of Béxar, Salcedo turned his attention to the business of his office. First, he commended Captain Varela for his conduct of affairs as lieutenant governor and relieved him of further responsibilities so as to allow the junior officer ample time to prepare for his reassignment to Presidio del Rio Grande.[95] Next, to dispel doubts and fears about the imperial structure, Don Manuel issued a proclamation to the provincial inhabitants informing them of the establish-

---

[94] For a comprehensive discussion of the election and its ramifications, see Nettie Lee Benson, "Texas Failure to Send a Deputy to the Spanish Cortes," *Southwestern Historical Quarterly*, 64, no. 1 (July, 1960), 16–35.

[95] Salcedo to Varela, Béxar, June 28, 1810, BA.

ment of a fifteen-member Council of Regency in Spain.[96] Later, on Monday, July 9, the governor, Bonavía, and other comrades-in-arms bade farewell to Captain Varela, after which Salcedo briefed the deputy commandant general on the relative weakness of Spanish forces in East Texas.[97] Then he listened to a petition by leading citizens of Béxar for armament and supplies with which to defend the capital in the event of aggression. Routinely, he notified his uncle of the meeting.[98]

In the summer of 1810 anxiety gripped frontiersmen in Spanish Texas. To intensify matters even further, Don Nemesio sent to Salcedo and Bonavía copies of a royal order requiring officers to contribute an unspecified percentage of their salaries to a war fund. The governor unequivocally objected to the measure. Bonavía, though, took an indirect approach. Acknowledging receipt of the decree, he reported on the poverty of the settlers and inquired what amount officers were expected to give.[99] Even more disturbing news received in Béxar from the commandant general pertained to an insurrection in faroff Caracas, information Bonavía promised to suppress lest misguided malcontents might be inspired to attempt a similar upheaval in Texas.[100]

What impact the knowledge of a South American revolt had on the composure of Hispanic stalwarts in Texas can only be surmised. Bonavía doubtlessly discussed the news with Salcedo and Simón de Herrera, governor of Nuevo León on extended duty in the province. Most likely Don Manuel told his colleagues of the rumors he heard in East Texas to the effect that dissatisfied Spaniards in Louisiana, assisted by Frenchmen and Anglo-

---

[96] Salcedo to the People of the Province, Béxar, July 1, 1810, BA.

[97] Bonavía to Commandant General [Nemesio Salcedo], Béxar, July 11, 1810; Salcedo to Bonavía, Béxar, July 10, 1810, BA.

[98] Salcedo to Señores Alcaldes *et al.*, Béxar, July 10, 1810, BA.

[99] Salcedo to Commandant General [Nemesio Salcedo]; Bonavía to [Nemesio Salcedo], Béxar, July 11, 1810, BA.

[100] Bonavía to Nemesio Salcedo, Béxar, July 11, 1810, BA.

Americans, were planning a revolt directed at New Spain. But rumors were not the same as overt deeds, although royalists in Béxar assuredly agreed that the border needed constant vigilance. During this period, presidial troops in Nacogdoches prepared for the mutual invasion of the Neutral Ground. Hence the three leading defenders in Béxar, conscious of the fact that in the past Hispanic Texas had withstood the pressures of crises, maintained an outward calm. Inwardly, however, they worried and waited as turbulent clouds gathered on the horizon.

One indication that Spanish guardians of pivotal areas braced themselves for difficult times was the improved mail service. Generally speaking, communication is vital to civilized people, and Hispanics in the Interior Provinces, allowing for handicaps of the day, kept themselves sufficiently well informed. Bonavía notified Salcedo that largely through the efforts of Antonio Cordero, on Wednesday, July 4, 1810, postal officials in Saltillo had established a weekly run to San Antonio de Béxar.[101]

Governor Salcedo, not forgetting his recent visit to the eastern border, briefly reviewed developments in that area. Of particular interest to him was the rapid depopulation. To offset the unchecked flow of inhabitants, on July 29, 1810, the Nacogdoches commander, acting on Don Manuel's orders, released a proclamation entreating Hispanic *émigrés* to return to Texas. As an inducement, he promised that he would strive to get approval for a progressive trading policy that would permit hard-working individuals to prosper and thus would improve the economic well-being of the province. To the men who feared arrest for one reason or another, the governor offered general amnesty in the name of the Spanish monarch; to foreigners he pledged that their cases would receive special consideration. Finally, he set Thursday, November 1, 1810, as the deadline before which fugitive

[101] Bonavía to Salcedo, Béxar, July 13, 1810; Cordero to Bonavía, Monclova, June 28, 1810, BA.

settlers could present themselves to royal officials who would restore their lands to them.[102] Indeed, at this critical moment in the
history of the province, Manuel María de Salcedo emerged as a
humanitarian. Regrettably, time and Don Nemesio worked
against the implementation of this grand design.

As a feeling of uneasiness permeated the Texas frontier, Hispanic authorities became more and more cooperative toward one
another. To be sure, at times high-ranking officers differed with
minor functionaries, but, in the main, responsible leaders worked
conjointly to safeguard the province from collapse. In mid-July,
to assist him with the task of examining the military units under
his command, Governor Salcedo, responding to orders from
Bonavía, commissioned the Béxar officer Cristóbal Domínguez as
inspector of troops.[103] To facilitate Domínguez' assignment, Don
Manuel instructed Father José Clemente Arocha, ecclesiastical
judge and member of the *isleño* aristocracy in the capital, to
allow the inspector to use as many administrative aides as he
needed.[104] If Salcedo and Bonavía, in light of renewed tension,
expected presidial reinforcements to arrive, Don Nemesio soon
disappointed them. In answer to a requisition of June 27, the
commandant general curtly replied that he had no means by
which to increase the number of officers, much less enlisted personnel, for Texas.[105]

On the eve of the expedition into the Neutral Ground by Spanish and United States troops, an operation planned in the spring
when Salcedo visited East Texas, the governor alerted his lieutenants to arrest anyone who dared to cross the border.[106] The

---

[102] Castañeda, *Our Catholic Heritage in Texas*, V, 431.

[103] Salcedo to Bonavía, Béxar, July 20, 1810, BA.

[104] José Clemente Arocha to Salcedo, Béxar, July 22, 1810, BA; Benson,
"Texas Failure to Send A Deputy to the Spanish Cortes," p. 24.

[105] Nemesio Salcedo to Bonavía, Chihuahua, July 24, 1810, BA.

[106] Salcedo to Commanders at Nacogdoches, Trinidad, Atascosito, and La
Bahía, Béxar, July 29, 1810, B.A.

precaution, of course, aimed at making a distinction between interlopers and *émigrés* who wanted to apply for resettlement under the provisions of Don Manuel's proclamation.

As Salcedo's commanders at all important crossroads anxiously watched the frontier for the slightest irregularity, Don-Nemesio began showing signs of truly wanting to assist his fellow officers in Texas. On August 6 he wrote a letter to his nephew Manuel informing him that arms for Béxar could be obtained from a Chihuahua factory at a cost of thirty pesos per weapon plus freight charges. He asked the governor to advise him on the number of rifles needed at the capital.[107] On the following day the commandant general addressed a communiqué to Bonavía, his chief representative for Texas and Coahuila, offering to sell fifty rifles at the price quoted Salcedo for use by the detachment at Saltillo. In this case, Don Nemesio made a concession in price: volunteer soldiers could purchase their weapons at a ten-peso discount.[108] That same day the elder Salcedo sent his nephew what amounted to a mild reprimand. He reminded the Texas governor that the royal resolution obligating Hispanic officers, except those engaged in active combat, to suffer a salary deduction, required no further comment from anyone.[109]

While these messages were en route to Béxar, Governor Salcedo sent a letter to his comrade-in-arms at Presidio del Río Grande, Mariano Varela, asking him to visit from time to time nearby Lipan Apache villages in search of branded horses stolen from Hispanic centers.[110] Then Don Manuel notified his uncle about plans for conducting a tour of inspection of the coast. Specifically, Salcedo asked the commandant general to designate the

---

[107] Nemesio Salcedo to Governor of Texas [Salcedo], Chihuahua, August 6, 1810, BA.

[108] Nemesio Salcedo to Bonavía, Chihuahua, August 7, 1810, BA.

[109] Nemesio Salcedo to Governor of Texas [Salcedo], Chihuahua, August 7, 1810, BA.

[110] Salcedo to Varela, Béxar, August 7, 1810, BA.

fund from which payment could be made to settlers who often accompanied the troops and served as interpreters.[111]

Unlike the inspection trip of early spring, preparations for the expedition to the Bahía settlement did not require extensive planning, probably because Béxar Hispanics now had a frame of reference, thus allowing officials time to devote to other administrative duties. Governor Salcedo, for instance, conceivably became annoyed when he learned that Gregorio Amador, the officer who assumed command of the Nacogdoches garrison during the interval of the Spanish–United States invasion of the Neutral Zone, had unavoidably delayed executing the loyalty oath because all presidial personnel except two were out on patrol.[112] If this bit of news was not bewildering enough, a few days later Bonavía received word from Trinidad that Captain Agabo de Ayala, the recently appointed commandant, had contracted a fever, which had weakened his strength. The ad interim leader and writer of the letter reported that he felt slightly feverish himself.[113] Governor Salcedo, unaware of what hindered his subordinates in the Sabine River sector, sent an urgent notice to the Nacogdoches commander imploring him to reinforce the settlement to withstand surprise attacks by Comanche Indians. In the event of such aggression, Don Manuel boldly promised armed support, but, recognizing the limited manpower available and the long distances involved, he ordered the garrison officer to warn travelers to restrict their movements so as not to provoke the hostility of the Indians.[114]

A more subtly ominous threat to the government in Texas than the feared Comanche menace was the expeditious manner

[111] Salcedo to the Commandant General [Nemesio Salcedo], Béxar, August 8, 1810, BA.

[112] Amador to Salcedo, Nacogdoches, August 10, 1810, BA.

[113] Felipe de la Garza to Deputy Commandant General [Bonavía], Trinidad, August 12, 1810, BA.

[114] Salcedo to Commander of Nacogdoches, Béxar, August 13, 1810, BA.

in which royalists processed two routine applications. The first request, submitted by Lieutenant Colonel Simón de Herrera to Bonavía, was for a passport for an obscure army captain in the neighboring province of Nuevo Santander, Juan Bautista de las Casas, who wanted to enter Hispanic Texas. The second petition, administered by Governor Salcedo and forwarded to his uncle for approval, was for a furlough for Antonio Sáenz, one-time officer in charge of Trinidad.[115] Texas loyalists little suspected that the existence they had known for so long would be shattered when the paths of the two applicants converged in Béxar. For the time being, Bonavía and Salcedo, understandably concerned but not necessarily frightened of the future, consulted one another on the publication of a document from Don Nemesio thanking enlisted personnel and officers for their voluntary contributions for the upkeep of the royal armies.[116]

One junior officer who gradually adjusted to the stresses of his new assignment on the Rio Grande was Mariano Varela. On August 18 he wrote to Bonavía discussing the question of sending out mounted patrols to police the Camino Real, a fact about which he also apprised Governor Antonio Cordero of Coahuila.[117] Shortly thereafter Captain Varela notified Manuel Salcedo that the Rio Grande presidio lacked a force large enough to make a thorough investigation of the Lipan Apache encampments in search of stolen horses. But even with a reduced number of men, Varela avowed that he would make every effort to obey the Texas governor's order.[118] Evidently the captain found himself in a position of not knowing exactly to which superior officer of which province he owed primary allegiance. Because of the

---

[115] Herrera to Bonavía, Béxar, August 14, 1810; Salcedo to Commandant General [Nemesio Salcedo], Béxar, August 20, 1810, BA.

[116] Salcedo to Bonavía, Béxar, August 14, 1810, BA.

[117] Varela to Bonavía, Presidio del Rio Grande, August 18, 1810, BA.

[118] Varela to Salcedo, Presidio del Rio Grande, August 20, 1810, BA.

vague geographic boundaries of the eastern Interior Provinces, Varela's outpost on the Rio Grande above Laredo easily fell within the overlapping termini of both Texas and Coahuila. Consequently Don Mariano again wrote to Bonavía asking that a corporal and six privates, most likely serving in Béxar, be returned to his detachment so that he could perform all regular duties and still be able to comply with Governor Salcedo's special orders.[119] Bonavía apparently ignored the petition, because a month later Varela reported that he still lacked troops for efficient service.[120]

Meanwhile, in San Antonio de Béxar new problems, stemming from Governor Salcedo's proclamation in Nacogdoches offering general pardon to runaway colonists, increased the strain on an overburdened frontier bureaucracy. Lieutenant Guadiana of Nacogdoches, back in East Texas from his recent expedition into the Neutral Ground, acquainted the governor with the fact than a Hispanic *émigré* had returned from Louisiana, the first fugitive settler to take advantage of the generous dispensation.[121] When Salcedo received Guadiana's letter, he belatedly informed Deputy Commandant General Bonavía of the amnesty proclamation and of the *émigré* who had asked for resettlement. More importantly, as tension increased on the borderlands, he petitioned Don Bernardo for advice on how to deal with repentant colonists.[122]

Since July 29, the day on which the Nacogdoches commander posted Salcedo's edict, the governor had surely deliberated the significant point that his unilateral decision had left him vulnerable to criticism by his superiors, especially Don Nemesio; this partly explained why he waited more than a month before

[119] Varela to Bonavía, Presidio del Rio Grande, August 22, 1810, BA.
[120] Varela to Bonavía, Presidio del Rio Grande, September 19, 1810, BA.
[121] Guadiana to Salcedo, Nacogdoches, August 24, 1810, BA.
[122] Salcedo to Bonavía, Béxar, September 3, 1810, BA.

telling Bonavía about it. Of course, other administrative problems—such as Varela's departure for the Rio Grande, the complicated election of a representative to the Spanish Cortes, diminishing manpower and matériel, and the forthcoming inspection tour of the coast—took up much of the governor's working day, but even then it seemed unnatural for him to neglect apprising his confidant in Béxar about this important decision. To be sure, the proclamation's subject matter, of and by itself, constituted an academic exercise, but with the appearance of the first fugitive settler in Nacogdoches it became an explosive issue to all Hispanic defenders on the frontier. Thus Salcedo squarely faced up to things when he finally told Bonavía about the procclamation as a method to stabilize the East Texas population.

Bonavía promptly replied that Don Manuel should honor petitions submitted under the provisions of the published proclamation; however, he left the entire matter to the governor's own judgment.[123] Clearly, Bonavía's firmness gave Don Manuel an opportunity to assert himself in the gubernatorial office. This fact notwithstanding, the two cavaliers continued to work closely in safeguarding the province. For instance, they disposed of some unfinished business, the solution of which had been pending since Salcedo's inspection in Nacogdoches, by utilizing revenue from the *mesteña* fund for the purpose of returning United States Army deserters to Louisiana.[124]

Once again Don Manuel prepared to leave the capital on an inspection trip. He informed his subordinate officers that, in his absence, Captain José Joaquín de Ugarte would be in charge of the government,[125] a fact that he also communicated to his uncle

[123] Bonavía to Salcedo, Béxar, September 4, 1810, BA.
[124] Bonavía to Commandant General [Nemesio Salcedo], Béxar, September 5, 1810, BA.
[125] Salcedo to Commanders of Trinidad, Atascosito, and Nacogdoches, Béxar, September 10, 1810, BA.

in Chihuahua, indicating that he expected to begin the tour on Wednesday, September 12, 1810.[126]

As planned, Manuel de Salcedo provisionally appointed Captain Ugarte as lieutenant governor of the province, after which he formally notified Bonavía of the assignment and left San Antonio de Béxar for the coastal settlement of La Bahía del Espíritu Santo.[127] There was no way for the Texas governor to know, as he rode away from the capital, that four days hence a parish priest in the remote Mexican village of Dolores would launch an insurrection against the viceregal government of New Spain that would ultimately touch the lives of Hispanic Texans who valiantly guarded an almost forgotten frontier.

[126] Salcedo to Commandant General [Nemesio Salcedo], Béxar, September 11, 1810, BA.

[127] Salcedo to Bonavía, Béxar, September 12, 1810, BA.

4. SOCIAL CONDITIONS IN HISPANIC TEXAS, 1808—1810

As THE FIRST DECADE of the nineteenth century unfolded, Hispanic Texans, seemingly unaware that international politics had reduced the province to a mere pawn on the diplomatic chessboard, pursued an almost prosaic existence that manifested itself in various facets of frontier life. Apart from the major responsibilities of colonial officials, the social problems that confronted Spanish settlers in Texas before the outbreak of the Hidalgo revolt of 1810 at times were serious, at others comical, and sometimes even pathetic. Broadly speaking, these problems ranged from routine civil administration, including the general behavior of the citizenry, to the unavoidable church and military affairs.

The vicissitudes of the Spanish bureaucracy at all levels involved paper. Hence the availability of stamped paper from the royal monopoly, aside from the intent of an official to use it, often determined the swiftness or tardiness with which the system functioned. In Texas frontier officers frequently attributed their dereliction of duty to a lack of stamped paper with which to report their earnest desire to comply with standing orders that they failed to execute because of insufficient means to carry them out. Paper, therefore, was a vital item in the Interior Provinces, and it constituted a recurring theme in the colonial administration of Hispanic Texas.

Not surprisingly, in San Antonio de Béxar, the provincial capital, there never seemed to be a shortage of paper. In fact, minor officials punctually informed the governor whenever they received their regular allotment.[1] In contrast, on such outer margins of the province as the Sabine River salient, frontier captains, who occasionally displayed initiative in offering suggestions for improving communications from their posts to the center, often found their plans thwarted by a scanty supply of paper. The commander of Trinidad, for instance, reported to Governor Manuel Salcedo that, to make future references easier, he would number all his correspondence.[2] All the same, in discharging his administrative obligations, he evidently became so engrossed with the numbering procedure that in less than one year he exhausted his paper allotment. Consequently, he petitioned his superior to reimburse to him the cost of three reams of paper.[3] An official in a neighboring western province advised the governor of Texas that illness and a lack of stamped paper had retarded his business correspondence.[4]

The commander of Trinidad, after writing more than 150 letters, later aroused the wrath of the governor by breaking the numerical sequence of his communiqués from East Texas. Spe-

---

[1] Juan Francisco de Collantes to Salcedo, Béxar, November 2, 1808, Béxar Archives, Eugene C. Barker Texas History Center, The University of Texas at Austin. Hereinafter cited as BA.

[2] Prietto to Salcedo, Trinidad, January 6, 1809, BA.

[3] Prietto to Salcedo, Trinidad, January 6, 1810, BA.

[4] Tomás Pérez to Salcedo, Monclova, January 5, 1810, BA.

cifically, Salcedo reprimanded him for carelessness in ascribing the number 188 to a letter when the preceding one bore the number 184![5] A change of command at the Trinidad outpost in no way altered the problem of paper. After Agabo de Ayala, the new commander, assumed his duties, he informed military leaders in Béxar that he needed paper for official correspondence. Three months later, apparently reconciled to the slowness of the bureaucracy, the Trinidad captain resubmitted his requisition.[6] Pedro López Prietto, the former commander of Trinidad recalled to the capital for the purpose of auditing his accounts, was more fortunate than his successor; he received payment for one and one-half reams of paper.[7] Not so successful with either requisitions or reimbursements was a third commander assigned to Trinidad, who shortly after news of Hidalgo's revolt reached Texas lamented that he had not submitted his reports because he lacked paper.[8]

While the personnel at distant outposts constantly suffered privations from inadequate supplies with which to defend the integrity of the empire, administrators in San Antonio de Béxar exercised little abstinence in claiming whatever provisions the commandant general of the Interior Provinces irregularly sent to Texas. Judging from the voluminous correspondence that emanated from the capital from its founding to the end of the colonial period, one can safely surmise that paper was not an article high-ranking officers prudently utilized. Illustrative of this assertion is selected correspondence between the governor and various individuals concerning proper administrative procedures.

---

[5] Prietto to Salcedo, Trinidad, June 5, 1810, BA.

[6] Agabo de Ayala to Salcedo, Trinidad, July 3, 1810, October 6, 1810, BA.

[7] Cordero to Salcedo, Béxar, December 25, 1808; Prietto to Salcedo, Béxar, August 28, 1810, BA.

[8] Felipe de la Garza to Salcedo, Trinidad, November 23, 1810, BA.

Early in March, 1809, the governor authorized a Béxar official, José Flores, to purchase an account book in which to record the municipal funds.[9] During the same month the commandant general, in a reply to a previous petition, denied the governor the privilege of hiring a secretary, a point that the superior officer reiterated later with a second refusal.[10] Disappointed but not altogether discouraged, Governor Salcedo, hoping to avoid another confrontation with his uncle but equally determined to assert himself in office, accepted the application from a capital resident who sought employment as an *escribano*.[11] The elder Salcedo prolonged making a decision on the question for nearly ten months. Finally he explained to the governor that, independent of the merits of the applicant, a depleted treasury precluded the hiring of a notary public for Béxar.[12] All the while, the Texas executive, trying to resolve an annoying predicament, availed himself of the clerical services of Anselmo Pereyra, a local militiaman. Amusingly, whenever the situation permitted, Salcedo, with unabashed inner satisfaction, no doubt, casually reminded his uncle that in Pereyra's absence from the capital the governor's office was without a secretary.[13] The commandant general, however, remained officially silent on the subject.

Considering the strained relationship between uncle and nephew, or possibly in spite of it, the governor's intermittent, uncompromising attitude toward his subordinates is understandable. For instance, in January, 1810, he reprimanded the officer at Atascosito, a post in East Texas renowned for its inacessibility in rainy weather, for not including sufficient information in offi-

9 Salcedo to José Flores, Béxar, March 3, 1809, BA.
10 Nemesio Salcedo to Salcedo, Chihuahua, March 20, May 1, 1809, BA.
11 Francisco Barrera to Salcedo, Béxar, March 24, 1809, BA.
12 Nemesio Salcedo to Salcedo, Chihuahua, January 22, 1810, BA.
13 Salcedo to Commandant General [Nemesio Salcedo], Béxar, March 1 [?], 1810, BA.

cial communiqués. Moreover, to impress the frontier captain with the necessity of submitting complete reports, Salcedo returned the letters to Atascosito.[14] On another occasion, to the commander of Nacogdoches, where conditions were increasingly tense owing to the proximity of the United States, the governor forwarded basic rules to be consulted by town authorities in preparing civic documents, especially those records pertaining to land.[15] So determined was Salcedo to achieve uniformity in his administration that he even dispatched instructions for filing deeds and mortgages to the judges in the capital.[16] Unfortunately, the governor, in his zeal to improve the bureaucracy, failed to contend with the whims of provincial lawyers, who either ignored the suggested guidelines or broadly interpreted their provisions. In any event, within two weeks the attorneys created so much confusion that Salcedo chastised them for obstructing the administrative process. To correct an untenable situation, he declared that all documents except those arranged by four government appointees were invalid,[17] a decision that precipitated an additional expenditure for paper. A single index of mortgages, deeds, powers of attorney, sales, and miscellaneous transactions, covering a nine-month period in 1819, necessitated forty-three pages.[18]

Representative of the administrative problems that constantly required the attention of Texas officials was the management of the postal system. In addition to such inevitable obligations as recruiting qualified personnel and transmitting accounts of collections and disbursements,[19] the operation of the mail service

[14] Salcedo to Commander of Atascosito [José Antonio Aguilar], Béxar, January 19, 1810, BA.

[15] Salcedo to José María de Guadiana, Béxar, January 4, 1810, BA.

[16] Salcedo and Clerks to Judges and their Jurisdictions, Béxar, March 4, 1810, BA.

[17] Salcedo, Béxar, March 17, 1810, BA.

[18] [Index], February 13–November 27, 1810, Béxar, BA.

[19] Tomás Flores to Salcedo, Béxar, April 15, 1809; Salcedo to Rafaél Mar-

in the field was exceedingly perplexing to Hispanic administrators. From the Trinidad outpost, a frontier leader dutifully notified the governor that floods had delayed the postal riders, but that he had issued orders for improved service.[20] Notwithstanding the Trinidad commandant's probable resourcefulness and the impact that inclement weather had on postal distribution, provincial authorities in either Saltillo, Chihuahua, or Béxar decided all important questions regarding the mail run. Periodically officials in these three locations, in an effort to promote better service, changed the departure-arrival schedule of the couriers. In the summer of 1810, for example, the mail to East Texas settlements went out every alternate Wednesday, whereas the residents in Béxar enjoyed a weekly delivery from Saltillo.[21] To safeguard the integrity of the system in the sweeping expanse between Béxar and the Sabine River, however, Governor Salcedo instructed the senior officer at Nacogdoches to adhere strictly to the mail schedule and, as an added precaution, to assign two soldiers to escort the mail carrier.[22] The governor of Coahuila introduced a similar policy for protecting the riders who traversed the royal road from Monclova to Béxar.[23] All the same, the Texas executive now and then modified the schedule in an attempt to coordinate more effectively the arrivals and departures of the couriers.[24] Hence, except for unforeseen delays, the incoming mail generally arrived in the capital from the neighbor-

---

tínez de Abal, Béxar, May 2, 1809; Bernardo Amado to Salcelo, La Bahía, February 18, March 18, 1810, BA.

   [20] Prietto to Salcedo, Trinidad, January 12, 1810, BA.

   [21] Andrés de Mendivil to Bonavía, [Saltillo], May 19, 1810; Prietto to Salcedo, Trinidad, June 1, 1810; Bonavía to Mendivil, Béxar, June 12, 1810, BA.

   [22] Salcedo to Guadiana, Béxar, July 2, 1810, BA.

   [23] Cordero to Bonavía, Monclova, July 7, 1810, BA.

   [24] Salcedo to Guadiana, Béxar, July 16, 1810, BA.

ing Interior Provinces to the west on Wednesday, and the out-going dispatches left on the following Saturday.[25]

Workable as it appeared at first glance, the arrangement was not without setbacks. Apart from variable factors—such as the dependability and horsemanship of the riders, the stamina of the mounts, and the condition of the highway—that indeterminably affected the system, the problem involved foibles in human character. Admittedly, the Spaniards in Texas possessed no monopoly on petty weaknesses. Yet their predilection for external ceremony, a tendency more noticeable in a frontier society than in a permanently settled community, heightened the effect of the shortcomings. On one recorded occasion in August, 1810, the mail carrier with the outbound post disrupted the apparent orderliness of the system when he failed to meet the rider with the incoming dispatches at the appointed place, probably a site somewhere between the Frio and Nueces rivers. The governor, in a lengthy explanation of the mishap, attributed the disorder to a careless observance of the new schedule.[26] Indeed, if the problem of merely getting the mail through seemed perplexing enough, the commandant general compounded the issue even further when, approximately a month later, he reminded Texas officials that a royal decree obliged mail service personnel who negligently or accidentally lost horses or mules to reimburse the government for the loss of such livestock.[27] Clearly the management of the post office department constituted an unending source of complaints and hindrances,[28] but it also reflected a significant aspect of Hispanic society in Texas.

[25] Bernardino Vallejo to Salcedo, Mission San José [Béxar], July 21, 1810, BA.

[26] Salcedo to Mendivil, Béxar, August 8, 1810, BA.

[27] Nemesio Salcedo to Bonavía, Chihuahua, September 5, 1810, BA.

[28] Martínez de Abal to Bonavía, Saltillo, September 5, 1810, BA.

If the operation of postal affairs at times created frustration for the upholders of royal authority in Texas, the administration of a military hospital was a source of unceasing concern. The hospital, situated on the grounds of the secularized Mission San Antonio de Valero, first opened its doors to patients on January 1, 1806. In addition to a superintendent, the staff included a physician, an orderly, a cook, and one servant.[29]

The idea of establishing hospitals in the northern borderlands probably originated with Felipe de Neve in 1783 when he became commandant general. Although he strongly urged the erection and maintenance of infirmaries in which the wounds and diseases of frontier troops could be treated, Neve's recommendation remained dormant,[30] at least in Texas, until the middle of the first decade of the nineteenth century. At the time of the establishment of the hospital in San Antonio de Béxar, Salcedo's predecessor described the equipment in these words:

I have had it [the hospital] provided with beds made of reeds (bamboo or cane stalks) in order to avoid the dampness of the ground. The patients of all companies or posts who may be sent here will be placed in them under the necessary care of a nurse (male), a woman to take care of the kitchen and [a] guard of the company of the Alamo which is stationed in that mission. The only expense entailed will be the increase of the troops' one *real* and a half per day to two *reales* and the remuneration of the doctor and cost of medicine.[31]

Quite often the infirmary needed improvements. Approximately one year after its founding, the governor instructed a local craftsman to obtain enough lumber to construct "thirty beds fully equipped." Subsequent to the fulfillment of this order and

---

[29] Carlos E. Castañeda, *Our Catholic Heritage in Texas: 1519–1936*, V, 409.
[30] Pat Ireland Nixon, *The Medical Story of Early Texas: 1528–1853*, p. 69.
[31] Cordero to Nemesio Salcedo, Béxar, October 19, 1805, BA; quoted in Nixon, *Medical Story of Early Texas*, p. 70.

just prior to Salcedo's arrival in Texas, the governor issued a new mandate calling for "the construction of two rooms in the abandoned mission of Valero, to the end that they may serve as the pharmacy for the military hospital." And so in piecemeal fashion the repairs continued. In February, 1809, the hospital physician, Jayme Gurza, advised the provincial government that further repairs were imminent, especially to the perforated roof of the building. Not surprisingly, the wheels of the Texas administration turned slowly until on May 2 Governor Salcedo, fully cognizant of the problem, instructed the hospital superintendent to inspect the premises and to submit his recommendations.[32] Within three days, the governor received the following report:

It [the roof] threatens to ruin the building. . . . All the rooms must be unroofed because all the shingles and beams are rotten, and 496 [iron bars] must be replaced because they are crumbling and rotting. The floors in the rooms and corridors of the infirmary upstairs and downstairs must be repaired. The chinks in all the walls, inside and outside, must be filled with small rocks and mortar. The corners of the north rooms, . . . must be [torn] and rebuilt. A new wall must be raised for the rooms facing the east, for it is completely deteriorated. The roofing and the gutters must be rebuilt because they are rotten and useless.[33]

The urgency of the superintendent's report prompted Salcedo to solicit the assistance of "an intelligent architect" in Chihuahua. Moreover, he unequivocally declared that, prohibitive as the entire cost of the renovation might seem to budget-minded superiors, the overall value of the hospital in terms of services rendered fully justified its immediate repair. With uncommon speed, higher authorities approved his request. Accordingly, while construction at the hospital progressed, the patients, save

[32] Nixon, *Medical Story of Early Texas*, pp. 72–73.
[33] Mariano Varela to Salcedo, Béxar, May 5, 1809, BA; quoted in Nixon, *Medical Story of Early Texas*, p. 23.

the ambulatory cases, convalesced at the residence of a widow, Doña Concepción. By the beginning of 1810, work crews finally completed the major restoration of the hospital, and the patients returned to their former, but now more livable, quarters.[34]

During Manuel de Salcedo's incumbency, the hospital physician encountered numerous difficulties in obtaining supplies. For instance, in 1808 he complained of the unserviceable condition of the moss-stuffed mattresses. Moreover, the doctor was appalled at the fact that only fourteen of the thirty beds had sheets. Yet the commandant general, inclined to dispense words, at least, freely, warned Texas officials to purchase "only the very urgent supply of materials." And so, when winter firmly gripped the town, the hospital superintendent mended six worn-out mattresses and "stuffed them with wool." Harsh as frontier conditions were, it took the Chihuahua authorities three years to understand "that mattresses and sheets were necessary equipment in a hospital." It was not until September of 1811, when threatened by the peril of an internal revolt, that the commandant general authorized the procurement "of five mattresses, 50 pairs of sheets and 30 blankets."[35]

When the hospital admitted its first patients in 1806, five came from the garrison at the capital and thirteen arrived from the other presidios. From time to time the number of patients varied, but quite likely it never exceeded the thirty-bed limit, although undoubtedly there was a waiting list. More numerous, of course, were the diseases and injuries the physician treated: gunshot and arrow wounds, fractures, smallpox, pneumonia, malaria, measles, influenza, syphilis, and gonorrhea. Initially only soldiers enjoyed the privilege of the hospital services, but by 1809 the authorities permitted charity cases—principally civilians attached to the Béxar garrison—to seek treatment. The nonmili-

[34] Nixon, *Medical Story of Early Texas*, p. 73.
[35] *Ibid.*, pp. 71–75.

tary inhabitants who entered the infirmary were not actually welfare patients. They paid a nominal fee of one *real* per day plus an additional charge for medication.[36]

Compared with other problems surrounding administration of the hospital, the task of procuring medicines was not particularly irritating. In fact, drug requisitions received expeditious consideration in the bureaucratic process. Somewhat annoying, however, were the unpredictable delays in delivery. Nevertheless, when medical supplies arrived at the capital, the infirmary staff dispensed them according to patients' needs and to reliable promises from the military high command that additional supplies would be forthcoming. The drugs frequently used at the Béxar hospital included gum opium, gum camphor, oil of anise, oil of cinnamon, white magnesia, sulphur, mercury, ointment, senna, epsom salts, and ipecac.[37]

Independent of the quality and quantity of the drugs and the professional competency with which the staff administered them is the question of the percentage of the population that benefited from these services. In the absence of conclusive testimony and considering the frontier environment, it seems plausible that Spanish Texans who sought medical attention received brief diagnoses of ailments that they attempted to cure later with home remedies—or died trying. Yet by another standard, the maintenance of a hospital, in spite of inadequacies, demonstrated a sense of compassion and commitment on the part of the government for the welfare of the governed. That the achievement came late in the colonial period is of secondary consequence. More significant is the fact that the Spaniards actually made the effort in the first place—especially in an area they traditionally neglected.

Corresponding in an administrative sense with the operation

[36] *Ibid.*
[37] *Ibid.*

of the hospital, but with distinct characteristics, were the non-technical problems pertaining to the military establishment and interrelated with other aspects of social life. In the spring of 1809, Governor Salcedo, while planning an inspection tour of the province, ordered the officials at La Bahía presidio to conduct a lengthy investigation into a reported theft of goods from the army storehouse.[38] The implication of the directive was twofold: either criminals ran rampant in the coastal area or the military personnel had relaxed their security measures. In any event, the high command instructed the governor to enforce stricter discipline at La Bahía.[39] So concerned was Salcedo with what he judged to be a breakdown in public order that he proposed to his uncle the construction of a new prison. The commandant general, however, aside from requesting cost estimates,[40] displayed little interest and tacitly disapproved the project. The governor, preoccupied with other administrative problems, never revived the proposal.

One issue to which the governor devoted much time was effective utilization of soldiers. In February, 1810, noting that most members of a 150-man detachment at Trinidad lacked weapons, he recommended reassigning all unarmed personnel to a public works detail in Béxar to construct barracks.[41] Although the suggestion received prompt approval, the arrival of an arms shipment in East Texas nullified the planned transfer of troops.[42] Temporarily nonplused, Governor Salcedo again pursued the idea of constructing new billets for the army. The commandant general, evidently in full agreement with the proposal, author-

[38] Salcedo, Francisco Vásquez, Simón de Herrera, et al., La Bahía, March 15–December 4, 1809, BA.
[39] Cordero to Salcedo, Béxar, March 22, 1809, BA.
[40] Nemesio Salcedo to [Salcedo], Chihuahua, January 8, March 16, 1810; Salcedo to Nemesio Salcedo, Béxar, February 8, 1810, BA.
[41] Salcedo to Bonavía, Béxar, February 16, 1810, BA.
[42] Bonavía to Salcedo, Béxar, February 17, 1810, BA.

ized the expenditure of funds for rehabilitating an old warehouse into suitable barracks for approximately 300 men,[43] possibly at La Bahía, where the need was most critical.

But in spite of the officials' intellectual commitment to the project, the plan quickly became tangled in the administrative thicket. Inevitably orders emanated from San Antonio de Béxar to the commander at La Bahía instructing him to submit cost sheets.[44] Before long the municipal authorities speculated on the probability that no one at the coastal settlement was sufficiently familiar with stonework techniques to prepare the necessary report.[45] Shortly thereafter, to the chagrin of the officers at Béxar, the commander at La Bahía forwarded a detailed statement that plunged the hierarchy into endless deliberation,[46] all of which delayed the actual construction. As a result of the copious correspondence back and forth, the commandant general, who had tentatively approved the project, returned the cost estimates to Béxar and warned his subordinates that it was imprudent to proceed with the plans without competent stonemasons.[47] Bernardo Bonavía, deputy commandant general in Texas, whose opinions commanded considerable respect in Chihuahua, anticipated such an objection and informed the governor's uncle that he had already considered the possibility of inviting a master builder to supervise the work at La Bahía. A week later Bonavía asked Governor Salcedo to suggest someone for the special assignment.[48]

[43] Nemesio Salcedo to [Salcedo], Chihuahua, April 2, 1810; Nemesio Salcedo to Bonavía, Chihuahua, May 18, 1810, BA.

[44] Varela to Bonavía, Béxar, April 21, 1810, BA.

[45] Bonavía to [Salcedo], Béxar, April 24, 1810, BA.

[46] Agabo de Ayala to Bonavía, La Bahía, April 28, 1810; Varela to Bonavía, Béxar, May 14, 1810; Salcedo to Bonavía, Béxar, May 14, 1810; Bonavía to Commandant General [Nemesio Salcedo], Béxar, May 16, 1810; Nemesio Salcedo to Bonavía, Chihuahua, May 19, 1810, BA.

[47] Nemesio Salcedo to Bonavía, Chihuahua, June 12, 1810, BA.

[48] Bonavía to Commandant General [Nemesio Salcedo], Béxar, June 13, 1810; Bonavía to Salcedo, Béxar, June 23, 1810, BA.

Evidently the supreme command in Chihuahua pondered the advisability of employing José María Caballero, an experienced architect, but hesitated on reaching a final decision. In turn, Bonavía, obviously in desperation, boldly suggested an alternate plan. Instead of spending money for the construction of a barracks Bonavía preferred organizing a corps of experienced frontier fighters. Unhappily, the suggestion earned him a stinging reprimand from the commandant general.[49] And so closed this aspect of an army problem, one that clearly showed that in Hispanic Texas worthwhile enterprises originating in a whirlwind of words often perished in a hot gust.

In the realm of church-state relations, the Salcedo administration moved erratically. The province of Texas fell under the spiritual jurisdiction of the bishop of Nuevo León,[50] but the responsibility for the regulation of cemeteries and the construction and maintenance of parochial churches rested with secular authorities.[51] Still, in the performance of duties affecting the church, the political leadership generally deferred to the wishes of the episcopal office.[52]

Locally, the Texas royalists enjoyed pleasant relationships with the clergy, especially with the padres stationed at the missions. In fact, Governor Salcedo at times intervened in the administration of ecclesiastical matters in an effort to retain meri-

---

[49] Nemesio Salcedo to Bonavía, Chihuahua, July 10, August 6, 1810, BA.

[50] Nettie Lee Benson (ed. and trans.), *Report that Dr. Miguel Ramos de Arizpe Priest of Borbon, and Deputy in the Present General and Special Cortes of Spain for the Province of Coahuila One of the Four Eastern Interior Provinces of the Kingdom of Mexico Presents to the August Congress on the Natural, Political, and Civil Condition of the Provinces of Coahuila, Nuevo León, Nuevo Santander, and Texas of the Four Eastern Interior Provinces of the Kingdom of Mexico*, p. 12.

[51] Salcedo to Clemente de Arocha, Béxar, December 15, 1808; Herrera to Arocha, Béxar, October 29, 1808, BA.

[52] Salcedo to Primo Feliciano Marín de Porras, Béxar, March 22, 1809; [Salcedo] to Arocha, Béxar, January 14, 1810, BA.

torious clerics in the province. For instance, in May, 1810, he persuaded the commandant general to use his influence to extend the tenure of a Franciscan friar assigned to Mission San José, Father Bernardino Vallejo, instead of allowing the religious superiors to promote the priest to a college presidency at Zacatecas.[53]

At other levels, however, the relationship acquired a different hue. Unwittingly, perhaps in a misguided attempt to assert the supremacy of the army over the frontier religious communities, the military high command occasionally strained the relations between the civil authorities and the clergy. In the summer of 1810 the commandant general notified the Texas provincial officers that a fund had been established for the purpose of purchasing candles to be used in soldiers' weddings.[54] Probably the decree stemmed from the fact that as early as 1808 the bishop of Nuevo León, as a precautionary measure against accidental fire, had "prohibited the use of an excessive number of candles . . . on the altars of churches." [55] Whether or not the commandant general, for morale purposes, wished to distinguish the weddings of Texas troops by providing additional candles cannot be determined; in any case, the decree from Chihuahua implied that, because of the existence of the fund, priests who officiated at military weddings could not charge a stipend, however nominal, for accessories used at the altar. At most the decree was an entering wedge, as subsequent events proved. In less than a month a new directive circulated in San Antonio de Béxar expressly prohibiting chaplains from charging anything for marriages, burials, or

[53] Salcedo to Nemesio Salcedo, Nacogdoches, May 6, 1810; Council of the Apostolic College of Our Lady of Guadalupe at Zacatecas to Nemesio Salcedo, [Zacatecas], June 30, 1810, BA.

[54] Nemesio Salcedo to Bonavía, Chihuahua, July 21, 1810, BA.

[55] Nettie Lee Benson, "Bishop Marin de Porras and Texas," *Southwestern Historical Quarterly*, 51, no. 1 (July, 1947), 37.

baptisms.[56] In a military unit stationed at the secularized Mission Valero, the unpleasant task of enforcing the decree fell to the company commander.[57] Fortunately, a compromise arrangement, which encouraged voluntary contributions,[58] restored relations to normal.

Despite the embarrassment of the donations controversy, Governor Salcedo continued to enjoy good rapport with the Franciscans. As a matter of fact, the College of Our Lady of Guadalupe in Zacatecas held the governor in high esteem for his support of Franciscan missionary activity.[59] Not so enjoyable, however, was Salcedo's relationship with the bishop of Nuevo León, Primo Feliciano Marín de Porras. The governor's unpleasant experience with the prelate began in 1809 when the Texas executive ordered Marín de Porras to submit a full account of an episcopal tour, conducted four years earlier, and particularly of the allegedly suspicious travelers who accompanied the bishop along the Camino Real from Nacogdoches to San Antonio de Béxar and even beyond.[60] The breach widened in a dispute involving a clergyman of low rank in Béxar of whom the governor disapproved. Appalled at Salcedo's audacity, Marín de Porras complained to Francisco Xavier Lizaña, archbishop of Mexico and, as a result of factional struggles, interim viceroy of New Spain. Essentially, the bishop of Nuevo León contended that Salcedo had repeatedly insulted him: "I suffer daily from the new governor of Texas, the absolute despotism with which he disposes

[56] Salcedo to Bonavía, Béxar, August 13, 1810, BA.

[57] Captain of Company to Salcedo, San Carlos de Parras [Béxar], August 18, 1810, BA.

[58] Bonavía to Salcedo, Béxar, August 20, 1810, BA.

[59] Council of the Apostolic College of Our Lady of Guadalupe at Zacatecas to Bernardino Vallejo, [Zacatecas], September 7, 1810, BA.

[60] Benson, "Bishop Marin de Porras and Texas," pp. 24–31.

at will my priests, holding them in shameful oppression, by boast-
ing of and broadcasting their weaknesses."[61]

Actually, the only clergyman whom Salcedo had publicly denounced was Juan Manuel Zambrano, subdeacon of San Fernando Church and a man of questionable virtue. In fact, shortly
before Salcedo's arrival in Texas, Zambrano had indulged in so
many worldly pleasures that he was in exile for several months
from the province. Yet because of his minor status in the clergy,
he secured permission, over the vehement protests of the new
governor, from the audiencia of Guadalajara to return to Texas.[62]
So opposed was Salcedo to the subdeacon's reappearance in the
provincial capital that he had him arrested and lodged in the
local jail. In retaliation, the bishop of Nuevo León excommuni-
cated the governor! Harsh as the ecclesiastical pronouncement
seemed, the prelate allowed Salcedo thirty days in which to make
proper restitution to the injured party. On November 27, 1809,
after the Texas official had fulfilled all conditions, Marín de
Porras absolved him "without delay in order to prove to him my
desire for the best unity and for the well-being of the people."[63]

To be sure, the excommunication of Governor Salcedo was an
unnerving experience for the victim. Irrespective of personal
anxiety, though, the episcopal decision represented the nadir of
church-state relations during Manuel de Salcedo's incumbency.
And yet the protagonists, by ameliorating a tense situation that
displayed the trappings of a major power struggle, showed that
men of strong mind and gentle conduct could resolve their differences in the interest of the empire they served. Nonetheless,
like other problems, the confrontation between the governor and

[61] *Ibid.*, p. 36.

[62] J. Villasana Haggard, "The Counter-Revolution of Béxar, 1811," *Southwestern Historical Quarterly*, 43, no. 2 (October, 1939), 225 n.

[63] Benson, "Bishop Marín de Porras and Texas," pp. 36–37.

the bishop provided impetus for one more inundation of stamped paper on an overburdened system.

Taken as a whole, the principal social questions in Texas reflected the broader spectrum of frontier life in the Spanish borderlands. After a century of colonization, the provincial government, from the center to the outermost settlement, maintained a benevolent paternalism toward all aspects of society. Hardly a single problem passed unnoticed, because neither the colonists nor the officials possessed the temperament to make such allowances. It seemed, in most instances, that troublesome difficulties motivated the bureaucracy into regulating even the minutest issues. The inhabitants looked hopefully to the government for solutions to everyday situations; to do otherwise seemed unnatural. Thus, in a sense, the administration of Manuel María de Salcedo formed the weft and the people he governed, the warp, of the social fabric of Hispanic Texas in the days before the Hidalgo revolt.

5. IMPACT OF THE HIDALGO
REVOLT UPON HISPANIC TEXAS

IT TOOK SEVERAL WEEKS before Texas royalists learned that on Sunday, September 16, 1810, Father Miguel Hidalgo y Costilla had launched a revolutionary struggle to end Hispanic political domination. The rebels professed loyalty at the outset to King Ferdinand VII, in whose interests they felt competent to govern and to protect the purity of Catholicism. They avowed that only American-born inhabitants knew intimately what was best for tottering New Spain, now called Mexico.

From the Indian village of Dolores, seedbed of the cataclysmic movement, the agitation spread outward in several directions. Initially Hidalgo's motley forces—known as the Army of America—experienced one triumph after another until Spanish troops checked their advance on the threshold of Mexico City. Retreating northward the haphazardly organized rebels broke up into armed bands led by men with or without ideas. These leaders generally agreed that without foreign assistance their only hope for success lay in revolutionizing the Interior Provinces, after which outside support might be obtained. To one of Hidalgo's chief lieutenants, Mariano Jiménez, fell the task of overturning the Hispanic structure in Coahuila and Texas.[1] Of the two provinces, Texas was the coveted goal because of its proximity to the United States, from where aid could be procured.

Slowly at first, then gathering momentum, the spirit of unrest permeated the northeastern borderlands. Guardians of Spanish Texas, unaware of the early stages of the insurrection, at best stiffened their token defenses; at worst they fatalistically waited for whatever the future held in store for them. By the end of October, 1810, Hidalgo agents, approaching closer to Texas, inflamed the Rio Grande settlements.[2] Indeed, Texas provincials presently found themselves confronted by fiery revolts south of the Rio Grande and east of the Sabine River in Louisiana. Late in September Anglo-American frontiersmen, inspired by events in Mexico and unobstructed by the government in Washington, attacked Baton Rouge, the colonial capital of Spanish West Florida, ousted the royalists, and inaugurated a short-lived republic that soon annexed itself to the United States.[3]

In the meantime, Governor Salcedo of Texas, apparently ignorant of the momentous events that shook the center of the viceroyalty, proceeded to La Bahía del Espíritu Santo, where he ordered the inhabitants to present documentation that indicated the lands to which they were entitled.[4] Moreover, he instructed the garrison commander to draft a report on the agricultural

[1] Hubert Howe Bancroft, *History of North Mexican States and Texas,* IV, 102–240, cited in Julia Kathryn Garrett (ed.) "Letters and Documents: Dr. John Sibley and the Louisiana-Texas Frontier, 1802–1814," *Southwestern Historical Quarterly,* 48, no. 1 (July, 1944), 69 n.

[2] J. Villasana Haggard, "The Counter-Revolution of Béxar, 1811," *Southwestern Historical Quarterly,* 43, no. 2 (October, 1939), 222.

[3] Dumas Malone and Basil Rauch, *The Republic Comes of Age, 1789–1841,* p. 126.

[4] Salcedo to Settlers of La Bahía, Béxar, September 16, 1810, Béxar

yield of the area and, more importantly, his personal impressions of the settlers' attitude toward the royal government.[5] Seeking to tap every source of intelligence, Don Manuel asked a local clergyman for details concerning both the management of church expenses and the political conduct of the faithful.[6]

As Salcedo acquainted himself with conditions at the coastal presidio, the commandant general in Chihuahua, responding to the emergency caused by the Hidalgo revolt, dispatched an important message that altered the defensive posture in Texas. To be precise, Don Nemesio, undoubtedly with much soul-searching, finally commissioned his nephew as full-fledged governor of the province and recalled Bernardo Bonavía to Durango.[7] Because of the revolutionary turmoil, the courier in all probability avoided traveling through rebel-held territory; thus the commandant general's latest order did not arrive in Béxar until mid-October.

That Hispanic leaders in Texas were uninformed about the Mexican insurrection is evident from a petty controversy revived by Governor Salcedo. A year earlier the governor had banished from the province a pleasure-loving subdeacon of San Fernando Church, Juan Manuel Zambrano. Now, late in September, 1810, Manuel de Salcedo in an injudicious moment, but likely remembering the unpleasant confrontation with episcopal authority that resulted from the incident, threatened the *audiencia* of Guadalajara with his resignation if the subdeacon returned to Texas.[8] Shortly afterward the governor conveyed similar pro-

---

Archives, Eugene C. Barker Texas History Center, The University of Texas at Austin. Hereinafter cited as BA.

[5] Salcedo to Commander of La Bahía [Andrés Mateos], La Bahía, September 25, 1810, BA.

[6] Salcedo to Bro. José Miguel Martínez, La Bahía, September 25, 1810, BA.

[7] Nemesio Salcedo to Governor of Province of Texas [Salcedo], Chihuahua, September 28, 1810, BA.

[8] Salcedo to the Judges of the Royal Audiencia of Guadalajara, La Bahía, September 29, 1810, BA.

tests on the matter to Bonavía and to the bishop of Nuevo León.[9] The controversy apparently ended when Bonavía at once assured the governor that he would prevent any scandal from erupting should Zambrano reenter the province.[10] As later events proved, other considerations soon demanded so much of the Spanish defenders' time that they forgot the dispute. Ironically, in the crises that followed the subdeacon turned out to be one of the staunchest royalists in the capital.

In faroff Chihuahua, Don Manuel's uncle sent another communiqué, which, in effect, nullified the Texas governor's Nacogdoches proclamation of amnesty to fugitive colonists. The commandant general, understandably suspicious of irregular movements and fearful of the consequences if they remained unchallenged, ordered his nephew to arrest the *émigrés*.[11] Furthermore, in a subsequent directive Don Nemesio warned Governor Salcedo to prevent conspirators and seditious individuals from entering the province.[12] But the commandant general was unaware that the first reports to reach Texas of the Hidalgo uprising had disturbed the uneasy tranquility in the Sabine River sector, causing many Hispanic settlers to flee across the border into Louisiana. The loss of the civilian population of East Texas would undermine the military posts in the area. Moreover, a flight would indicate a loss of faith in Spanish arms and in the governor's ability to defend the province. On the other hand, revolutionists bent on overturning the Hispanic regime constituted a serious threat to dedicated royalists who were convinced of the righteousness of the king's cause.

---

[9] Salcedo to Bonavía, La Bahía, October 8, 1810; Salcedo to Primo Feliciano [Marín de Porras], La Bahía, October 8, 1810, BA.

[10] Bonavía to Salcedo, Béxar, October 9, 1810, BA.

[11] Nemesio Salcedo to Governor of Texas [Salcedo], Chihuahua, October 2, 1810, BA.

[12] Nemesio Salcedo to Governor of Texas [Salcedo], Chihuahua, October 3, 1810, BA.

At La Bahía, by the first week in October, Governor Salcedo, surely cognizant of the agitation launched by the padre of Dolores, apprehensively notified Bonavía in Béxar about Hispanic migration out of East Texas. Alarmed by these new developments, Don Manuel implored the deputy commandant general to suggest a workable plan to curtail the depopulation.[13] Illustrative of the anxiety that troubled the governor was a reprimand he sent to the officer in charge in Nacogdoches for permitting a woman to escape to Natchitoches where she sought refuge.[14] More in harmony with his benevolent policy for keeping settlers in East Texas, however, Salcedo instructed the Nacogdoches commander to advise two men who applied for readmission that, if they responded within five days after being notified, a pardon would be forthcoming.[15] Exactly how Governor Salcedo reacted when he received his uncle's order countermanding the Nacogdoches proclamation is difficult to ascertain, but surely he must have been perplexed when a follow-up decree from Don Nemesio, dated October 13, 1810, rescinded the first counterorder. In effect, the commandant general allowed Salcedo's proclamation to stand.[16]

By mid-October Spanish protectors of the borderlands appeared exceedingly worried by the inroads that insurrectionists had made into the northeast. Don Nemesio, in particular, was unusually inclined toward consulting his subordinates and searching every avenue of possible assistance, even outside support. To Diego Murphy, Hispanic consul in New Orleans, the commandant general sent a request for cooperation in obtaining arms in

[13] Salcedo to Bonavía, La Bahía, October 5, 1810, BA.
[14] Salcedo to Commander of Nacogdoches [Guadiana], La Bahía, October 5, 1810, BA.
[15] Governor of Texas to Commander of Nacogdoches [Guadiana], La Bahía, October 6, 1810, BA.
[16] Nemesio Salcedo to Governor of Texas [Salcedo], Chihuahua, October 13, 1810, BA.

the United States, a plan perhaps suggested by Governor Salcedo in response to the earlier warnings of the envoy from Spain, Luis de Onís.[17] Next, he ordered his nephew Manuel to acquire munitions from the neighboring nation; under heavy guard he shipped twenty thousand pesos for that purpose. Possibly to conceal the apprehension that clutched the bureaucracy, the commandant general asked the Texas governor to select a trusted individual for the special mission to Louisiana, someone other than experienced officers, such as Simón de Herrera or Cristóbal Domínguez, whom he vitally needed in the Interior Provinces.[18] The implication of Don Nemesio's decision was clear. Every knowledgeable observer who assessed the progression or regression, as the case might be, of the revolt realized that Texas was the corridor to the United States. Therefore, if agents for either the protagonists or antagonists should succeed in obtaining armaments, the prestige of the Anglo-American nation could be linked to their cause. Thus no last-minute inspiration caused the commandant general to look hopefully beyond the Sabine River. Rather, he had at last correctly appraised the significance of Texas' geographic position and was belatedly endeavoring to reinforce a staggering structure.

To encourage the support of the royalists, to reassure the doubtful, and certainly to win back misguided rebels, Don Nemesio issued a lofty proclamation citing the cherished values and benefits of the past. He unleashed his wrath specifically on Napoleonic emissaries who conspired with disgruntled Hispanic-Americans to confuse and divide the allegiance of the inhabitants.[19]

[17] Nemesio Salcedo to Diego Morphy [*sic*], Chihuahua, October 13, 1810, BA.
[18] Nemesio Salcedo to Governor of Province of Texas [Salcedo], Chihuahua, October 13, 1810, BA.
[19] Nemesio Salcedo to Inhabitants of his Jurisdiction [Chihuahua], October 13, 1810, BA.

Having decided on a course of action, Don Nemesio started to pull his top officers out of Texas. Already he had dispatched an order recalling Bernardo Bonavía to his former assignment in Durango. In fact, the deputy commandant general, after communicating the news to Governor Salcedo at La Bahía, acknowledged the mandate and expressed his regret to his superior for not having accomplished more at the command post he was leaving.[20] As Bonavía arranged to repair to Durango, Don Nemesio sent a directive to Lieutenant Colonel Simón de Herrera to report to Chihuahua.[21]

During these exchanges Governor Salcedo evidently sensed the crucial status of frontier administration, just as he was about to assume full control. His principal officer in Nacogdoches, José María Guadiana, soon notified him that more settlers had applied for readmission into Texas under the terms of the July proclamation.[22] For Don Manuel the perennially unsettled state of affairs in East Texas constituted only one problem, but presumably he took consolation in knowing that at least the Hispanics in that sector had begun to respond to his offer. Notwithstanding this apparent success, other essential issues, all requiring immediate attention, mounted in intensity. As the revolutionary menace threatened the southwestern periphery of Texas, the governor recognized the necessity for returning to the provincial capital; from there he could direct matters with renewed confidence. And so, in anticipation of his planned departure from the coastal settlement, Salcedo issued a proclamation to the Bahía populace imploring them to behave worthily as loyal subjects of the king.[23]

Back in Béxar, Manuel de Salcedo and his fellow royalists

[20] Bonavía to Commandant General [Nemesio Salcedo], Béxar, September 17, 1810, BA.

[21] Nemesio Salcedo to Herrera, Chihuahua, October 16, 1810, BA.

[22] Guadiana to Salcedo, Nacogdoches, October 19, 1810, BA.

[23] Salcedo to Settlers at [La] Bahía, La Bahía, October 21, 1810, BA.

girded themselves for a persevering struggle to defend the system they served. On Thursday, October 25, among the first tasks that the governor discharged was to commission José de Rossi as special representative on an arms-buying run to Louisiana,[24] an assignment that the *vecino* accepted the next day.[25] Within a short period a treasury official in Saltillo, acting on orders from Don Nemesio, notified Salcedo that ten boxes containing twenty thousand silver pesos with which to purchase the weapons and ammunition were en route to Béxar.[26]

During the last week of October Governor Salcedo took firm command of the situation at the Texas capital. Judging from the voluminous correspondence that went out on Friday, October 26, Don Manuel must have availed himself of the services of an *escribano*. First, he wrote to his subordinate at the Atascosito outpost asking for his cooperation in halting the spread of the insurrection.[27] Next, he dispatched a set of instructions to Félix Trudeaux, Spanish vice-consul at Natchitoches who worked in accord with Diego Murphy of New Orleans, to support Rossi on the munitions-buying trip to the United States.[28] Then, leaving

[24] Salcedo to Josef de Rossi [*sic*], Béxar, October 25, 1810, BA.

[25] Rossi to Salcedo, Béxar, October 26, 1810, BA.

[26] Manuel Royuela to Salcedo, Saltillo, October 25, 1810, BA.

[27] Salcedo to Commander at Atascosito [Aguilar], Béxar, October 26, 1810, BA.

[28] Philip C. Brooks, "Spain's Farewell to Louisiana, 1803–1821," *Mississippi Valley Historical Review*, 27, no. 1 (June, 1940), 39; Salcedo to Trudeau[x], Béxar, October 26, 1810, BA. As early as the previous July, Félix Trudeaux had offered his assistance to Salcedo and had avowed that he held a commission from the Spanish consul in New Orleans. Evidently, Trudeaux and Salcedo knew each other, perhaps from the Texas governor's sojourn in Louisiana, because Don Félix frequently conveyed his personal regards to Don Manuel. In any case, during the 1810 summer crisis in East Texas the commandant general advised the Texas officials that, since communication across the Sabine River was prohibited, Trudeaux's services were unnecessary. Nonetheless, Salcedo and Bonavía in all probability failed to notify Trudeaux of Don Nemesio's directive, because Don Félix continued to correspond with Salcedo

no channel of possible assistance unexplored, Don Manuel asked for similar cooperation from Consul Murphy and Luis de Onís.[29] Finally, he cautioned the Nacogdoches commander to be extremely alert for an insurgent attack.[30]

Moreover, to prop up East Texas' dubious security, Governor Salcedo transferred his special inspector of military affairs, Captain Cristóbal Domínguez, to oversee the entire periphery of defense, which extended from Nacogdoches to the Gulf coast, and to inspire loyalist troops who guarded the frontier against wanton aggression.[31] In sending Domínguez on this extraordinary assignment, Salcedo realized that the few officers with undermanned contingents were liable to be overrun by revolutionary hordes. Again he broached the subject of inadequate manpower in Texas to his uncle the commandant general. Rather than requesting reinforcements from elsewhere as he had in the past, the governor, obviously counting on the success of Rossi's pending mission to the United States, asked for authorization to enlist two hundred militiamen from the local gentry in Texas. To emphasize an important point, Don Manuel declared that, in addition to his gubernatorial duties, which were cumbersome enough, the threat of the Hidalgo revolt had placed even heavier obligations on the governor's office. Still, with Bernardo Bonavía preparing to return to Durango, Salcedo reassured the commandant general that

---

while the governor was at La Bahía. Coincidental with the outbreak of the Hidalgo revolt, Deputy Commandant General Bonavía sought to convince Don Nemesio of the vital need to communicate with Trudeaux in Natchitoches (Guadiana to Governor of Province of Texas [Salcedo], Nacogdoches, July 6, 1810; Felix Trudeau[x] to Salcedo, Natchitoches, July 27, 1810; Nemesio Salcedo to Bonavía, Chihuahua, September 3, 1810; Trudeau[x] to Salcedo, Natchitoches, September 28, 1810; Bonavía to Commandant General, [Nemesio Salcedo], Béxar, October 3, 1810, BA).

[29] Salcedo to Murphy, Béxar, October 26, 1810; Salcedo to Luís de Onís, Béxar, October 26, 1810, BA.

[30] Salcedo to Guadiana, Béxar, October 26, 1810, BA.

[31] Carlos E. Castañeda, *Our Catholic Heritage in Texas, 1519–1936*, V, 435.

presently he would himself assume command of the provincial troops. Just the same, the governor petitioned his uncle not to deny assistance should the rebellion reach Texas.[32]

Another example of how Manuel Salcedo, despite the scarcity of resources, tightened his defenses in the crisis precipitated by Padre Hidalgo was a plan conveyed to his former companion-in-arms, Antonio Cordero of Coahuila, which called for the use of passports by anyone traveling through the Interior Provinces. Within Texas proper, Don Manuel avowed that he would demand strict observance of this precaution.[33] Approximately two weeks later, Don Antonio replied from Saltillo, where he had taken refuge when insurrectionists jeopardized the safety of his capital at Monclova, that he concurred with the plan. He further suggested that letters should be sent only through the royal postal service.[34]

In this critical period Governor Salcedo, plagued by numerous problems, doubtlessly felt some relief of mind when, on October 24, Hispanic presidential soldiers negotiated a peace settlement with the belligerent Comanche chiefs; he promptly notified his uncle of the event.[35] But even as Indian depredations temporarily subsided on one front, royalists in Texas faced ever increasing dangers from the southwest. In late October Salcedo learned that revolutionists had allegedly sent two spies to murder all defenders of the king's cause. This disquieting report of an assassination plot he shared with his friend at Mission San José, Father Bernardino Vallejo. The news certainly must have shaken the governor's composure, but, as he apprised his informant, he had re-

[32] Salcedo to Nemesio Salcedo, Béxar, Letters 223, 225, 227, 228; October 27, 1810, BA.

[33] Salcedo to Cordero, Béxar, October 27, 1810, BA.

[34] Cordero to Salcedo, Saltillo, November 7, 1810, BA; Frederick C. Chabot (ed.), *Texas in 1811: The Las Casas and Sambrano Revolutions*, p. 23.

[35] Salcedo to Nemesio Salcedo, Béxar, Letter 227, October 27, 1810, BA.

doubled his efforts to uphold the Hispanic structure.[36] On Sunday, October 28, 1810, Salcedo formally assumed command of the Texas military forces as Bernardo Bonavía, in compliance with superior orders, departed from San Antonio de Béxar.[37]

Turning his attention briefly to East Texas, Don Manuel acquainted Guadiana of Nacogdoches with José de Rossi's special mission to Natchitoches and directed him to arrange suitable rest facilities prior to the agent's arrival.[38] On the last day of October, Rossi finally left Béxar on his assignment to Louisiana.[39] Two weeks later, upon entering Nacogdoches, Rossi found Guadiana waiting for him. The East Texas commander required the emissary to swear that he possessed no documents of a nature detrimental to the Spanish government; he then allowed the agent to cross the border.[40]

At the provincial capital Salcedo meanwhile calculated a few options open to him. First, he relieved José Agabo de Ayala of the Trinidad command post, because of his chronic illness, and assigned Felipe de la Garza.[41] Then, in anticipation that Rossi might fail in the mission to the United States, he dispatched an urgent requisition for war supplies to the Marqués de Someruelos in Cuba, pledging prompt cash payment once the shipment had been delivered safely on the Texas coast.[42]

From his headquarters in Chihuahua, the commandant general warned his nephew to search all travelers entering the prov-

[36] Salcedo to Governor of Nuevo León [Herrera], Béxar, October 28, 1810; Salcedo to Bernardino Vallejo, Béxar, October 31, 1810, BA.

[37] Bonavía to Salcedo, Béxar, October 28, 1810, BA.

[38] Salcedo to Guadiana, Béxar, October 28, 1810, BA.

[39] Salcedo to Nemesio Salcedo, Béxar, October 31, 1810, BA.

[40] Guadiana to Salcedo, Nacogdoches, November 16, 1810, BA.

[41] Salcedo to Commander of Atascosito [Aguilar], Béxar, October 29, 1810; Agabo de Ayala to Deputy Commandant General [Bonavía], Trinidad, September 28, 1810, BA.

[42] Salcedo to Señor Marcos [Marqués] de Someruelos, Béxar, October 30, 1810, BA.

ince so as to prevent the distribution of seditious literature.[43] In keeping with the spirit of this decree and certainly in harmony with the Salcedo-Cordero accord to restrict the conveyance of letters exclusively to the postal system, the governor discreetly instructed José Erasmo Seguín, postmaster at Béxar, to hold the incoming and outgoing mail pouches until Don Manuel could inspect them himself at the earliest opportunity. Until a more effective method of examination could be implemented, however, Salcedo asked Seguín not to disclose the procedure to the Béxar populace.[44] In fact, rebel aggression so disrupted the mail service south of the Rio Grande that the governor complained to the intendent of San Luis Potosí about the virtual impossibility of sending communiqués to Mexico City.[45] Concerned as he was about interruptions in the courier system to the viceregal capital, Don Manuel found occasion to improve his own mail center. Without delay, he instructed Seguín to maintain better order at the Béxar post office, but at the same time to allow for an examination of the pouches by either the governor or his representative. Furthermore, Salcedo directed army subordinates at all major river crossings—namely, the Guadalupe, San Marcos, Colorado, Brazos, and Trinity rivers—to record accurately the time of arrival and departure of the mail rider.[46]

As the winter season closed in, anxiety just short of panic gripped the Texas frontier. For protection, two guards were assigned to José Clemente Arocha, ecclesiastical judge of Béxar, whenever he had to walk about the town at night.[47] As a further precaution, Salcedo stationed troops around the government

---

[43] Nemesio Salcedo to Governor of Texas [Salcedo], Chihuahua, October 30, 1810, BA.

[44] José Erasmo Seguín to Salcedo, Béxar, November 6, 1810, BA.

[45] Salcedo to the Intendent of the Province of San Luis Potosí, Béxar, November 7, 1810, BA.

[46] Salcedo to Seguín, Béxar, November 8, 1810; Salcedo to Cordillera Commanders, Béxar, November 30, 1810, BA.

[47] Arocha to Salcedo, Béxar, November 10, 1810, BA.

buildings to prevent a surprise attack.[48] These developments hardly stymied Salcedo.

In the second week of November, the silver shipment from Chihuahua arrived in Béxar. The money must have restored the shaky confidence of capital guardians; they should have been thankful enough to overlook slight discrepancies. Yet, after careful inventory, Governor Salcedo and several witnesses, meticulously adhering to administrative detail, certified that the consignment, supposedly containing twenty thousand pesos, was sixty-two pesos short of the full amount.[49]

Aware that Don Nemesio had sent the money to pay for munitions from the United States, armaments he obviously intended to distribute throughout the northern borderlands, Governor Salcedo reminded his uncle that he still needed additional personnel and funds and again asked for authority to enlist local settlers in the defense of the province.[50] To be sure, security, an all-encompassing problem, required the closest cooperation between officials in Chihuahua and those in Béxar. Under normal conditions such cooperation was the case, but the Hidalgo revolt so complicated matters that Spanish defenders sometimes worked at frustrating cross-purposes. Generally speaking, the two Salcedos agreed on the necessity of procuring arms to crush the insurrection in the Interior Provinces. As the plan unfolded, the younger Salcedo performed the clerical duty and placed the prestige of his office behind the Rossi mission. Regrettably, before the culmination of the project, the Texas governor found himself in an embarrassing position; the commandant general, for undisclosed reasons, suggested that Don Manuel should forego the proposal to purchase firearms from Louisiana and should attempt to procure them from the nearby provinces of Coahuila, Nuevo

[48] Salcedo to Guardia de Govierno [*sic*], Béxar, November 10, 1810, BA.

[49] Salcedo *et al.*, Béxar, November 11, 1810, BA.

[50] Salcedo to Commandant General [Nemesio Salcedo], Béxar, November 11, 1810, BA.

León, or even Nuevo Santander.[51] With a simple stroke of the pen Don Nemesio thus undermined the Rossi mission to the United States.

With the passage of two months since the outbreak of the revolution, East Texas, as a peripheral area, resumed importance in the minds of Hispanic administrators. In the last week of October Governor Salcedo reminded his subordinate officer in Nacogdoches that November 1 was the expiration date of the amnesty proclamation. Until then the commandant possessed authority to permit former colonists to relocate in the province.[52] After the deadline, though, Salcedo charted a more stringent course. He ordered Guadiana to close the frontier to foreigners and to confine settlers to the immediate vicinity of their dwellings.[53] Presumably, the localization of inhabitants applied to all settlements in the province. The maintenance of security, given the circumstances of the turbulent period, was paramount.

Beyond the southwestern extremity of Texas royalist officers vigilantly guarded the highways and back trails. José Ramón Díaz de Bustamante, of the presidio at Laredo, informed Salcedo that as presidial commandant he possessed sufficient power to issue passports and to require people to carry unsealed letters, with the single exception of a special permit that travelers were obliged to present to army commanders at different outposts. In deference to Don Manuel's wishes, however, Díaz de Bustamante promised that he would not allow anyone, save muleteers, to enter Texas.[54]

In view of the magnitude of the revolutionary challenge to royalist authority, Governor Salcedo briefed his uncle on the

[51] Nemesio Salcedo to Governor of Texas [Salcedo], Chihuahua, November 13, 1810, BA.

[52] Salcedo to Guadiana, Béxar, October 28, 1810, BA.

[53] Salcedo to Guadiana, Béxar, November 14, 1810, BA.

[54] José Ramón Díaz de Bustamante to Salcedo, Laredo, November 16, 17, 1810, B.A.

preventive measures he had initiated in the province, principally the careful inspection of the mail and the restriction of settlers to the communities of their residence.[55] Curiously, the commandant general, who usually reprimanded his Texas officials for not assuming a firmer stance, later countermanded his nephew's security decrees because they were too strict.[56] Be that as it may, Manuel Salcedo, for the time being unconcerned about his uncle's vacillating tendencies, conducted his governorship in the manner that he felt best served the king's interests, namely as a holding action.

Consequently, in the latter part of November Don Manuel clarified his stringent policy to the provincial governor of Nuevo León. First, he curtailed the distribution of personal mail in Texas. Second, he allowed business correspondence to be dispatched unsealed. Third, he required official mail to be delivered promptly to its destination. And last, he prohibited civilians, unless they justified the need, from traveling about in the province.[57]

At the end of November an urgent communiqué from the viceroy of New Spain, dated September 27, 1810, finally reached Salcedo in Béxar. Almost immediately the governor conveyed the news to his trusted frontiersmen: Father Hidalgo and two confederates, Ignacio Allende and Juan Aldama, might invade Texas on their way to the United States. Unacquainted with conditions in Texas, the viceroy nevertheless asked Hispanic Texans to capture the rebels.[58] Salcedo found himself in a quandary. Because of the unreliability of the courier system through

[55] Salcedo to Commandant General [Nemesio Salcedo], Béxar, November 19, 1810, BA.

[56] Nemesio Salcedo to Governor of Texas [Salcedo], Chihuahua, December 11, 1810, BA.

[57] Salcedo to Governor of Nuevo León [Herrera], Béxar, November 21, 1810, BA.

[58] Viceroy to Salcedo, Mexico City, September 27, 1810; Salcedo to Cordillera Commanders, Béxar, November 29, 1810, BA.

rebel-held territory south of the Rio Grande, Don Manuel sent a letter to Félix Calleja, high-ranking general in charge of the viceregal forces, through the dependable coordination of Antonio Cordero of Coahuila. When Salcedo's letter apprising Calleja of Texas' defenseless position arrived in Saltillo, Don Antonio quickly replied that he would suspend forwarding it until he knew for certain where the loyalist general could be located.[59]

In an effort to tighten control over the fringe areas, Salcedo reaffirmed his order to Guadiana in Nacogdoches not to grant authorization to settlers who wished to visit Béxar unless they could demonstrate cause for making the trip.[60] All the while, Guadiana cautiously observed the inhabitants in his jurisdiction. The captain reported to the governor that soldiers deployed at all vulnerable positions were equipped with the limited matériel available. Since a number of men lacked flints for their firearms, however, he urged Salcedo to furnish these vital items at an early date, a requisition Don Manuel promised to fulfill shortly.[61] With respect to the problem of forbidding settlers to go to Béxar, Guadiana dutifully published Salcedo's prohibition of travel decree, but he seriously questioned the prudence of enforcing it.[62]

Without doubt, the defensive framework of Texas creaked at the joints. The new commander at Trinidad, in charge of 127 men, stated that his armory was short; he needed 291 flints and 4,776 cartridges in order for his soldiers to have sufficient expendable equipment.[63] Salcedo himself lamented that he needed

[59] Salcedo to Félix Calleja, Béxar, November 21, 1810; Salcedo to Cordero, Béxar, November 21, 1810; Cordero to Salcedo, Saltillo, November 27, 1810, BA.

[60] Salcedo to Guadiana, Béxar, November 22, 1810, BA.

[61] Guadiana to Salcedo, Nacogdoches, Letter 379, November 22, 1810; Salcedo to Guadiana, Béxar, November 29, 1810, BA.

[62] Guadiana to Salcedo, Nacogdoches, Letter 381, November 22, 1810, BA.

[63] De la Garza to Salcedo, Trinidad, November 23, 1810, BA; Chabot, *Texas in 1811*, p. 22.

more horses for the cavalry units to replace the mounts that had stampeded.[64] Gradually the governor's patience wore thin. After repeatedly asking his uncle for permission to enlist militiamen and getting no reply, he contacted Cordero about the possibility of recruiting two hundred Lipan Apache warriors. To open negotiations with the Indians, at least, Salcedo sent a friendly Lipan and an interpreter to confer with Díaz de Bustamante at Laredo.[65] The governor had no way of knowing, except through trial and error, whether this approach would produce results at all—and in the end nothing came of the move—but the significance is that in an emergency he kept probing for pragmatic solutions.

In the midst of the crisis, which had caught Hispanic Texans hopelessly unprepared, Manuel de Salcedo issued an edict relating to the celebration of the feasts of the Immaculate Conception and the Virgin of Guadalupe, both of which occurred in December. The lengthy proclamation indicated that not even the threat of a rebel invasion could persuade Spanish Christians to postpone a socioreligious function to which they were accustomed.

Justly wishing [decreed Salcedo] to afford this settlement the annual diversion of the feasts they customarily celebrate during the days of Our Lady of the Concepción [December 8] and Our Lady of Guadalupe [December 12], and to see to it that the celebrations are held in a most decorous manner because of the critical circumstances of these days, I shall dictate the following provisions designed to furnish amusement for everyone with peace and the prevention of the evil intentions of disturbers of the public peace.

For these reasons the following rules shall be observed:

1st. The bazaar booths and the bullring shall be located in one of the plazas to be selected by the feast-day committee and the city

[64] Salcedo to Manuel Royuela, Béxar, November 28, 1810, BA.
[65] Salcedo to Díaz de Bustamente, Béxar, November 29, 1810, BA.

attorney. They shall be placed in the best order possible and shall leave ample room for the traffic and recreation of the public.

2nd. During the days when no festivities or sanctioned games are being held, the bazaar shall be closed at the sound of retreat. . . .

3rd. From tonight [Sunday, December 2] forward taps shall be sounded from the Parish church of this *villa* one hour after retreat. This signal will indicate that no one shall be about in the streets without a legitimate reason. . . .

4th. The days of public festivities and sanctioned games shall be the following:

The 7th, from vespers in the evening until 12 o'clock that night, at which time the bell will be rung for taps in order that everyone may retire to his home and all the bazaar booths may be closed. . . .

The 8th, the 9th, the 10th, the 11th, and the 12th until the afore-cited hour.[66]

Especially revealing were the references to the Hidalgo revolt, passages that pointed out how Hispanic defenders frantically tried to combat what to them was an elusive evil:

5th. Whenever this government office may be compelled for some just reason to suspend the customary celebration for the purpose of preventing a serious disturbance caused by some perturber of public peace, it shall make it known setting forth the cause that impels it to take such action. The desire I have to contribute to the satisfaction of the settlers cannot be the cause of my neglecting my sacred obligation to preserve this province from the fatal destruction of the revolution which has engulfed certain settlements in the viceroyalty. It may be justly feared that the revolutionary leaders may have some partisans here, although I do not believe that any such perditious monster can be found among us because of the loyalty of the inhabitants of this province.

6th. Likewise, I hereby order the members of the municipal coun-

---

[66] Proclamation of Manuel de Salcedo, Béxar, December 2, 1810, in Walter Prescott Webb (ed.), "Texas Collection: Christmas and New Year in Texas," *Southwestern Historical Quarterly*, 44, no. 3 (January, 1941), 358–359.

cil and the wardbosses to watch and preserve good order and public tranquility; the former shall assign themselves the districts they are to patrol, and the latter shall do the same with their respective wards. All of them shall immediately arrest any one found drunk or anyone disturbing the peace in order that respectable persons may amuse themselves in peace.[67]

As preparations for the celebration went forward, a report by a townswoman who claimed to have sighted an unknown officer prowling the backstreets of Béxar deepened the atmosphere of doubt and suspicion. Capital administrators quickly launched a two-day investigation, which resulted in endless confusion.[68] Assuredly, the fear of a thrust from the south kept royalists in a state of agonizing uncertainty. Through it all, Salcedo's perseverance manifested itself in his relationship with high-level bureaucrats. On December 4, after a delay of more than six weeks, the governor finally acknowledged Don Nemesio's order recalling Simón de Herrera out of Texas. Instead of meekly submitting to superior rank, however, Salcedo convincingly argued that, with Bonavía's recent reassignment to Durango, there was only one other experienced frontiersman who could assist the Texas executive in holding the province safely for the crown— Lieutenant Colonel Herrera. Therefore he appealed to the commandant general to reconsider the decision.[69] In this instance the elder Salcedo yielded to his nephew's request and allowed Don Simón to remain in Texas.

With so much depending on José de Rossi's ability to fulfill his commission, Hispanic royalists in Béxar undoubtedly wondered how the purchasing agent had fared in the United States. By December 6, Rossi, with nothing substantial to report, merely

[67] *Ibid.*
[68] Joaquín de Ugarte to Salcedo *et al.*, Béxar, December 3–4, 1810, BA.
[69] Salcedo to Commandant General [Nemesio Salcedo], Béxar, December 4, 1810, BA.

informed the governor of his arrival at Los Rápides, a small community near Fort Claiborne in central Louisiana.[70] Success, however minimal, seemed to elude the royalists in their quest for survival. Nemesio Salcedo, troubled by news of the insurrection that erupted east of Louisiana, authorized the Texas governor, so as to save precious time in sharing intelligence information, to open any correspondence from the United States addressed to the commandant general. Concerning the question of enlisting a sizable number of militiamen, Don Nemesio merely promised to aid his nephew in the event of an extraordinary emergency.[71]

Because he had not heard from Rossi since mid-November, Governor Salcedo had decided, even before he received this communiqué, to send a follow-up mission to Louisiana. In selecting a new purchasing agent, Apolinar de Masmela,[72] Don Manuel clearly chose to ignore the commandant general's suggestion to abandon the idea of procuring war supplies in the United States.

Without much difficulty, Manuel María de Salcedo and his government withstood the pressures of the revolt for the rest of the year. On the day after Christmas the governor made a crucial decision that, in the short run, weakened the province's military defenses. To shore up the royal forces of his friend and former associate, the beleaguered Antonio Cordero of Coahuila, Don Manuel decided to return a hundred-man contingent, originally under the command of Salcedo's predecessor in Texas, to Saltillo. All the same, the Texas governor retained twenty-five soldiers from Cordero's unit and placed them on special duty at the different outposts in the province.[73]

For Hispanic Texas, the year 1811 began with the same strains

---

[70] Rossi to Salcedo, Los Rápides, December 6, 1810, BA.

[71] Nemesio Salcedo to Governor of Texas [Salcedo], Chihuahua, December 11, 1810, BA.

[72] Salcedo to Murphy, Béxar, December 15, 1810, BA.

[73] Salcedo to Nemesio Salcedo, Béxar, December 26, 1810, BA.

and stresses that had characterized the months following the outbreak of the Hidalgo uprising. The new year, though, introduced more ominous signs of unrest than ever before. To provide for the safety of his wife and daughter, the governor, with utmost secrecy, sent them to East Texas. When their absence became noted, speculation on their whereabouts intensified the anxiety of the populace.[74]

On the second day in January, Governor Salcedo assembled the troops of the Béxar garrison, three hundred strong, in the military plaza. Standing before them, he announced that presently they would repair to the Rio Grande from where they would defend the province more effectively. A cloud of gloom descended on the villa. Rumor-mongers quickly spread stories throughout the town; the most common held that Salcedo and Herrera planned to leave Texas defenseless to the mercy of the revolutionists and the Indians. No one felt secure in this apocalyptic atmosphere, least of all the soldiers whose primary duty was to provide protection.[75]

When he learned of the rumors, Governor Salcedo angrily issued a sharp denial. To counteract the gossip, on Sunday, January 6, he published a proclamation to the inhabitants of Texas, appealing for support of the royalist cause. In this decree he strongly denounced as unfounded the rumors that Spanish loyalist officers in the viceroyalty intended to abandon New Spain in deference to the demands of the French. Moreover, he cautioned the people to pay no heed to rebel propaganda that aimed at dividing the allegiance of the populace. Last, he urged them to remain steadfast in their backing of the Hispanic system of values under which they had lived for so long.[76]

[74] Carlos E. Castañeda, *Our Catholic Heritage in Texas, 1519–1936*, VI, 6 n. 13.
[75] *Ibid.*, VI, 6.
[76] *Ibid.*, VI, 5.

For the time being, Texas held the line against the insurrection. Across the Rio Grande, however, part of the royalist defenses collapsed. Antonio Cordero briefly engaged the enemy at an encampment called Aguanueva, but, when his own command defected to the rebel army, he surrendered.[77] One loyalist captain who escaped promptly wrote to Salcedo about the disaster and indicated his plan to withdraw to the Rio Grande, taking along funds and a few weapons.[78]

Following Cordero's capture, tension on the Texas-Coahuila frontier mounted. On Sunday, January 13, Salcedo of Texas sent communiqués in several directions. First, he ordered the governor of Nuevo León, Simón de Herrera, to position the Texan royalist forces so as to prevent the rebels from communicating with sympathizers in Louisiana.[79] Second, to Joaquín de Ugarte, who had served as lieutenant governor while Salcedo inspected La Bahía, Don Manuel promised an officer and a fighting unit of three hundred men to reinforce his defenses in the southwest. Furthermore, the Texas governor directed Captain Ugarte to take whatever measures were expedient—from impressing militiamen to commandeering horses—to halt the rebel advance.[80] To Díaz de Bustamante at Laredo Salcedo also dispatched an urgent plea to enlist settlers to fight the insurrectionists.[81] And finally, to the custodian of the royal treasury at Saltillo Don Manuel sent a request for him to save the money lest it should fall into the hands of the enemy.[82]

For two days an uneasy calm settled over Béxar. Then, on the night of Tuesday, January 15, rebel sympathizers led by an

[77] Chabot, *Texas in 1811*, p. 23.

[78] Sebastián Rodríguez to Salcedo, Monclova, January 9, 1811, BA.

[79] Salcedo to Governor of Nuevo León [Herrera], Béxar, January 13, 1811, BA.

[80] Salcedo to Ugarte, Béxar, January 13, 1811, BA.

[81] Salcedo to Díaz de Bustamante, Béxar, January 13, 1811, BA.

[82] Salcedo to Royuela, Béxar, January 13, 1811, BA.

escaped prisoner from a makeshift jail at Mission San Antonio Valero almost succeeded in toppling the Casas Reales. Fortunately Salcedo, Herrera, and other loyalists uncovered the plot and arrested the conspirators, including the leader, Lieutenant Antonio Sáenz, before they could execute the plan to seize the government.[83] In the wake of this alarming development, Governor Salcedo cancelled the marching order for the Béxar garrison. To him the provincial capital needed more protection than the Rio Grande settlements.[84]

On Friday, January 18, the governor called a special junta to which he invited representatives of the municipal council, the clergy, and the military. The purpose of the meeting was to formulate a concerted effort to suppress conspiracy and to strengthen the defensive perimeter of Béxar. The junta, after professing loyalty to the Spanish monarchy, endorsed the work of the governor and his close associate, Lieutenant Colonel Herrera. Apart from the oral and written declarations of the junta, designed to placate unrest and dissension, elsewhere the ideas of rebellion, effectively nurtured by propagandists, took firm hold of the minds of soldiers and civilians in the Texas capital.[85] The next day Governor Salcedo prepared a declaration to the citizens of Béxar urging them to take up arms in defense of the legitimate authority. To give aid and comfort to the rebels, he warned, was tantamount to treason. Since Hispanic administrators had the province's best interests at heart, he advised the people to place their trust in God and in the king's men.[86]

No matter how carefully the royalists laid their plans, the outcome, to a large extent, rested on the support of devoted troops. In past crises the Hispanic borderlands had withstood internal

[83] Castañeda, *Our Catholic Heritage in Texas*, VI, 6–7.
[84] Salcedo to Sebastián Rodríguez, Béxar, January 16, 1811, BA.
[85] Castañeda, *Our Catholic Heritage in Texas*, VI, 7.
[86] Salcedo to the People at Béxar, Béxar, January 19, 1811, BA.

and external threats because of the vitality of the Bourbon reforms that had reinvigorated the flagging defensive cordon. By
1811, however, the strength of the reforms was exhausted. There
seemed to be no way to insulate the army's fidelity from infec-
tious ideas of discord and rebellion. Fear, suspicion, distrust, and
disaffection so permeated the province of Texas, particularly at
the center, that it was only a question of time before a leader
stepped forth to deliver the *coup de grâce*.

Within the confines of San Antonio de Béxar, shrewdly await-
ing the opportune moment, there was such a leader—Juan Bautista de las Casas, a retired militia captain from Nuevo Santander.[87] Placing himself at the head of the local opposition to
Governor Salcedo's administration, Las Casas, on the night of
Monday, January 21, surreptitiously plotted with four disgruntled sergeants to overthrow the royalists early the next
morning. Using the enlisted personnel billeted in the Quartel, a
barracks complex in La Villita, as the mainstay of the movement,
Las Casas and his confederates marched before daybreak on
January 22 to the government building, where they arrested the
governor and his entire military staff. Even in such dire circumstances, Salcedo and Herrera maintained their dignity. As the
governor and the royalist officers retired to detention in the Casas
Reales, the rebel soldiers instinctively saluted them.[88]

After overthrowing the royalists, Las Casas, intoxicated with
power, plunged the province into deeper confusion by his rash
actions. With great rapidity he confiscated the property of Hispanic residents, proclaimed himself head of the provisional government, released political prisoners, jailed loyalists and sympathizers of the king's cause, rewarded a few of his closest supporters, and sent agents to revolutionize Nacogdoches, La Bahía, and

[87] Chabot, *Texas in 1811*, p. 24.
[88] Castañeda, *Our Catholic Heritage in Texas*, VI, 8–10; Richard G. Santos,
"The Quartel de San Antonio de Bexar," *Texana*, 5, no. 3 (Fall, 1967), 189.

other settlements and outposts in Texas. Last, he dispatched a communiqué to the insurgents in Coahuila informing them of the success of his revolt in Béxar, after which he waited for Hidalgo, who reportedly was en route to Texas, to recognize his accomplishment.[89]

The following month Las Casas, attempting to consolidate his position by removing all vestiges of royalism in Béxar around which opposition to rebel rule might coalesce, chained Salcedo, Herrera, and twelve other Hispanic officers and humiliated them in front of the townspeople. Afterward the usurper transferred the royalists under heavy guard to Monclova, where an insurrectionist band led by Pedro de Aranda confined them to a hacienda supposedly belonging to a former loyalist, Lieutenant Colonel Ignacio Elizondo.[90]

From San Antonio de Béxar the insurrection spread like a prairie fire throughout the rest of the province. Las Casas' chief lieutenant, Antonio Sáenz, encountered little resistance when he arrived in Nacogdoches. He promptly arrested the presidio commander, seized the public archives and treasury, and announced the collapse of the Spanish regime. The story was virtually the same at other East Texas outposts. Adherents to the Hispanic cause lost their property and liberty. Sáenz, with one swoop, overturned a tottering structure.[91]

Meanwhile, in Béxar, the initial flush of rebel victory bouyed Las Casas' self-importance. On February 27, 1811, he received two revolutionary agents—Field Marshal Ignacio Aldama and Father Juan Salazar—who, on orders from Mariano Jiménez in

[89] Haggard, "Counter-Revolution of Béxar, 1811," p. 225.

[90] *Alta traición contra Don Juan Bautista Casas capitán retirado por haber alzado la vos de la insurrección en esta San Fernando de Béxar a 22 de Enero*, Nacogdoches Archives, Texas State Library, Austin, Texas; Luis Castillo Ledón, *Hidalgo: La vida del héroe*, II, 188.

[91] Dr. John Sibley to William Eustis, Secretary of War, Natchitoches, February 9, 1811, Record Group 107, National Archives, Washington, D.C.

Saltillo, had stopped over at the Texas capital on their way to the United States, where they hoped to secure assistance for the Hidalgo movement. In no time at all, the arrogant manner in which Aldama strutted about town in a French uniform studded with decorations and gold braid antagonized the more conservative elements in society. Moreover, the hospitable reception Las Casas gave to the emissaries convinced some residents that the aims of the rebels did not coincide with the best interests of Texas. In fact, not a few loyalist sympathizers considered Aldama a Napoleonic agent.[92] Yet the actions of the two envoys, obnoxious as they were, shrank in comparison with Las Casas' arbitrary performance, which soon aroused a wave of criticism behind closed doors. In his seizure of power, Las Casas had obtained the backing of the lower social stratum and the rank and file of the army. As a leader, though, Las Casas indiscreetly ignored two important groups, the old-time officers and the *isleño* aristocrats, without whose support the flimsy foundation on which his rule rested could not endure for long.[93] Among those whom he alienated was Antonio Sáenz, a disenchanted rebel who had definite views about leaders and followers.

Opposition to Las Casas' regime gradually solidified around the leadership of the subdeacon of San Fernando, Juan Manuel Zambrano. From his ranch twenty leagues away, Zambrano kept himself fully informed on events in Béxar through his brothers, José Darío and José María, both of whom were ordained priests. During the last week in February, Zambrano quietly entered the capital and assumed command of the underground resistance to Las Casas. Next to the brothers Zambrano, the principal counter-insurgents included Captain Ignacio Pérez, José Erasmo Seguín, Juan Veramendi, and Francisco Ruíz. Before proceeding with the movement to oust Las Casas from power, the group leaders

92 Chabot, *Texas in 1811*, p. 25.
93 Haggard, "Counter-Revolution of Béxar, 1811," p. 226.

carefully engaged the support of influential citizens and army officers. Failing in an attempt to obtain the endorsement of the two rebel envoys, the opponents to the revolution met on the night of March 1 to complete their plans before Las Casas uncovered the plot against his government. As an indication of how well Zambrano organized the opposition, the group even duped Lieutenant Antonio Sáenz, now wholly alienated by the usurper, to spread disenchantment at the military barracks. By midnight the counterrevolutionists formed a governing junta, with Zambrano as president, which pledged fidelity to King Ferdinand VII and promised to restore the legitimate authority in Béxar. The decision undoubtedly shocked dedicated rebels like Sáenz, but he and others of the same ilk realized that the prospect of assisting Zambrano against Las Casas appeared more advantageous than continuing under the present regime. At sunrise on March 2, the procession to the government house reenacted the activities that had toppled a previous governor thirtynine days before. Las Casas, devoid of all support, surrendered without a fight. With the removal of Juan Bautista from office, the Zambrano-led junta reestablished royal control in Texas, arrested the rebel agents, and dispatched two trusted messengers to communicate the news to the commandant general of the Interior Provinces.[94]

The two riders from Béxar traversed a devious route, especially near Presidio del Rio Grande, until they reached the Coahuilan community of San Fernando. There they encountered royalist sympathizers who directed them to the Elizondo hacienda, where Governor Salcedo was held captive. In the interim, the Texas executive, suspecting that his captor had become disillusioned with the Hidalgo revolt, taunted the colonel with vague promises of professional advancement if he denounced the rebel-

[94] *Ibid.*, pp. 226–231.

lion in favor of royalism. The arrival of the two messengers from
Texas and the news they related to Salcedo convinced the misguided Elizondo to switch allegiance for the last time.[95]

On the night of Wednesday, March 13, Salcedo, Herrera,
Elizondo, the two riders from San Antonio, and José Menchaca,
a Hispanic Texan in exile, charted a plan by which they thwarted
Padre Hidalgo and his band of rebels. First in a series of fast-
moving events was the capture in Monclova, on March 16, of
Pedro de Aranda, custodian of important revolutionary documents that revealed to the royalists the route of travel chosen by
the insurrectionists on their march to the northeastern provinces.
Next, on March 21, was the concealed deployment of loyalist
fighters around the Wells of Baján, the site selected by Mariano
Jiménez for a rendezvous with Hidalgo; this resulted in the surprise apprehension of a sizable part of the Army of America,
including the entire high command.[96] Then Salcedo, inspired by
the successful outcome of the plan, left Herrera at Monclova
and, with a loyalist contingent, escorted the twenty-seven captured rebel leaders from Monclova to Chihuahua, headquarters
of the commandant general.[97] Finally, arriving at Chihuahua
after a grueling expedition, Governor Salcedo detailed a select
guard of one sergeant, one corporal, and fifteen soldiers to detain
the prisoners at the Royal Military Hospital, formerly a Jesuit
college.[98]

In response to viceregal prompting, on April 26, 1811, Nemesio
Salcedo appointed a seven-member military tribunal, with the
governor of Texas as president, to conduct the proceedings against
the revolutionaries.[99] With uncommon expediency, the court

[95] *Ibid.*, pp. 231–232.
[96] Carlos Pereyra (comp.), *Obras de D. Lucas Alamán: Historia de Méjico*,
II, 167–171. Hereinafter cited as Alamán, *Méjico*.
[97] Castillo Ledón, *Hidalgo*, II, 196–198.
[98] *Ibid.*, II, 204.
[99] *Ibid.*, II, 205–206.

concluded its findings against the accused and condemned them to be shot. The executions began in May and continued through the summer months. On June 26, two of Hidalgo's high confederates, Mariano Jiménez and Juan Aldama, faced the firing squad.[100] Ultimately, on Monday, July 29, after pronouncing the death sentence, the military board turned the principal instigator of the rebellion, Padre Hidalgo, over to an ecclesiastical court, which defrocked the cleric according to canon law in the Royal Military Hospital. In the crowded hallway, acting as a witness for the state, Manuel Salcedo of Texas watched the tense drama, flanked by his uncle and representatives of the secular and regular clergy. No observer who followed the proceedings doubted the outcome. The end came soon. The next day, Miguel Hidalgo y Costilla, reduced to the status of a layman by the clerical court, paid the supreme penalty for inciting an insurrection against the authority of the king of Spain.[101] For Governor Salcedo an unpleasant task was over, but an even more harrowing experience awaited him in Texas.

In San Antonio de Béxar, the governing junta of Subdeacon Zambrano administered the province in the absence of a duly designated official. Besides restoring royal control, the junta members provided for the inauguration of a primary school, regularized the sale and distribution of vital foodstuffs to prevent hoarding, and authorized the trading of Texas horses for rations and other supplies in Louisiana. On July 11, 1811, while Salcedo presided at the trial of the revolutionists in Chihuahua, the Zambrano committee proclaimed to the citizenry the end of its rule. Shortly thereafter, on July 13, Simón de Herrera, tired but triumphant, arrived in Béxar to assume provisional leadership of the province. In deference to the work accomplished by the junta, Don Simón courteously delayed accepting a formal

[100] Alamán, *Méjico*, II, 181–182.
[101] Castillo Ledón, *Hidalgo*, II, 235–240.

transfer of command until July 22.[102] In Nacogdoches Cristóbal Domínguez reestablished loyalist rule and carefully watched activities in the Neutral Ground.[103]

As an object lesson to the people of Texas not to rebel against royal authority, victorious loyalists in Coahuila judged, convicted, and executed the prisoners arrested in San Antonio de Béxar—the usurper Las Casas, Field Marshal Aldama, and Father Salazar. Furthermore, as a reminder of punishment adjudged to insurrectionists, Antonio Cordero, reinstated to power, shipped Las Casas' head in a box to Béxar, where soldiers displayed the gruesome object on a pole in the military plaza.[104]

On balance, the achievements of the redeemers of royalism in Texas constituted sufficient proof of their allegiance. The commandant general asked Herrera to furnish a list of worthy participants in the restoration of Hispanic rule in Béxar so that adequate recompense could be made to those individuals.[105] Accordingly, each junta member received proper commendation from Don Nemesio and a reward in the form of either a promotion or a cash remuneration. For example, the elder Salcedo elevated Subdeacon Zambrano to the rank of lieutenant colonel and raised the political status of San Antonio de Béxar from *villa* to *ciudad*.[106] Even Herrera won recognition for his role in capturing the rebels in Coahuila when the viceroy of New Spain promoted him to the grade of full colonel.[107] Ironically, only Salcedo remained under a cloud of doubt.

The resumption of the gubernatorial duties by Manuel María

[102] Haggard, "Counter-Revolution of Béxar, 1811," pp. 233–234.

[103] Nemesio Salcedo to the Provisional Junta [Committee] of San Fernando [de Béxar], Chihuahua, July 20, 1811, BA.

[104] Chabot, *Texas in 1811*, pp. 30–31.

[105] Nemesio Salcedo to Herrera, Chihuahua, August 1, 1811, BA.

[106] Haggard, "Counter-Revolution of Béxar, 1811," p. 234.

[107] Nemesio Salcedo to Governor of Texas [Salcedo], Chihuahua, October 28, 1811, BA.

de Salcedo became an irritating problem to the commandant general. In the opinion of the younger Salcedo, the Texas office had lost prestige in the Las Casas upheaval. He therefore requested what amounted to an inquiry by a military board into the events surrounding that disaster in Béxar. In short, he wanted an exoneration. Don Nemesio, in denying the petition, insisted that Las Casas simply had caught Salcedo off guard. Nonetheless, in view of the restoration of legitimate government, the commandant general felt that his nephew possessed sufficient power to deal with provincial affairs.[108] Disappointed by his uncle's indifferent attitude, Governor Salcedo returned to Béxar on September 11, 1811, but, apart from discharging Cristóbal Domínguez from the East Texas assignment because of complaints against the officer's conduct, he refused to assume his regular duties.[109]

Manuel Salcedo's defiance of Don Nemesio's orders forced the issue into clear focus: since the office of the governor of Texas had suffered a definite loss of prestige, only through a public recognition of services rendered to the Spanish crown would the people again respect the man who administered the province. After all, Nemesio Salcedo could afford the luxury of issuing wordy decrees from afar, but his nephew had to enforce them in an atmosphere where the *vecinos* remembered how rebels had disgracefully dragged him in chains through the streets. To some bureaucratic bystanders the dispute between the uncle and nephew may have appeared a bit trifling, but to a cavalier like Salcedo it was a question of honor.

As the quarrel between the Salcedos continued week after week, the commandant general eventually concurred with one of Don Manuel's decisions—the dismissal of Domínguez—but on terms dictated in Chihuahua. In compliance with the gover-

[108] Nemesio Salcedo to Herrera, Chihuahua, October 15, 1811, B.A.
[109] Salcedo to Nemesio Salcedo, Béxar, October 18, 1811, BA.

nor's report about Domínguez' unpopularity in East Texas, Don Nemesio transferred the border captain to the Rio Grande as subinspector.[110] Aside from that minor concession, the disagreement unceasingly dominated the exchange of correspondence between the two capital cities. Colonel Herrera, as ad interim executive, advised the commandant general of his willingness to obey a superior mandate, received on November 2, instructing him to transfer command of the province to Salcedo, but still Don Manuel remained adamant in his refusal.[111] Steadfast in his convictions, he futilely appealed to his uncle for a judicious settlement of his case:

> I am particularly sensitive about my reputation. At all times I have striven to merit the good opinion of my superiors by sacrificing my health and risking my life in the service of our Sovereign. My meager pay I have frequently contributed whenever it has been necessary for the benefit of the Crown. I have laid bare the feelings of my heart and I plead with you to lay aside all considerations of kinship in order that justice may be done to a loyal subject and faithful vassal of His Majesty in accord with his merits. It is not reward that I seek, but the satisfaction of being invested with the office of governor with the same public approval and honors as were granted to Antonio Cordero.[112]

Unsympathetic to Salcedo's plea and impatient with his continued disobedience, the commandant general informed Colonel Herrera that he had ordered Salcedo to assume the governorship without further delay.[113] Casting aside his nephew's objections, the elder Salcedo advanced an argument of his own: the very fact

---

[110] Nemesio Salcedo to Cristóbal Domínguez, Chihuahua, October 29, 1811; Salcedo to Nemesio Salcedo, Béxar, November 13, 1811, BA.

[111] Herrera to Nemesio Salcedo, Béxar, November 4, 1811, BA.

[112] Salcedo to Nemesio Salcedo, Béxar, November 4, 1811, BA; quoted in Castañeda, *Our Catholic Heritage in Texas*, VI, 41.

[113] Nemesio Salcedo to Herrera, Chihuahua, November 26, 1811, BA.

that higher authorities had allowed Governor Salcedo to return to Texas was ample proof that they trusted him for the assignment, and promotion or other compensations were therefore superfluous.[114] Anxious to get on with other matters, the commandant general dispatched a courtesy report to the viceroy, intended for publication in the *Gaceta de México*, that covered mainly the details of Zambrano's coup against the usurper Las Casas.[115] Simón de Herrera interceded with Don Nemesio by offering to comment on those statements prepared for publication which cited the roles played by prominent royalists, including Manuel Salcedo, in the counterinsurgency.[116] Don Nemesio silently ignored the offer.

The virtual immunity enjoyed by Subdeacon Zambrano, whose debauchery offended the governor, was particularly galling to Salcedo's royalist pride. In response to an old complaint, the *audiencia* of Guadalajara had informed the governor that he could treat Zambrano as he wished but it also cautioned Don Manuel that the worldly subdeacon had performed a valuable service to the crown in overturning the Hidalgo revolt in Béxar.[117] But personal insult, though certainly humiliating, contributed less to Salcedo's obstinance than did the erosion of his authority. The Texas governor's contention that without proper recognition of his work from higher echelons the populace would not readily accept his leadership became an unpleasant reality. A townsman in Béxar openly rejected a verbal directive, declaring that Don Manuel had to submit it in writing. Needled by this insubordination, Salcedo immediately arrested the man, but later, after re-

[114] Nemesio Salcedo to Salcedo, Chihuahua, November 26, 1811, BA.

[115] Nemesio Salcedo to Governor of Texas [Salcedo], Chihuahua, October 28, 1811, BA.

[116] Herrera to Commandant General [Nemesio Salcedo], Béxar, November 27, 1811, BA.

[117] Antonio de Villa Urrutia to the Governor of the Province of Texas [Salcedo], Guadalajara, December 3, 1811, BA.

considering the incident, he instructed the jailkeeper to release the prisoner at sunrise.[118]

To an extent, Salcedo's refusal to reassume his gubernatorial duties was itself insubordinate, but he acted according to the accepted Spanish practice of *obedesco pero no cumplo*. In this context, his behavior implied that, although he fully understood the magnitude of superior orders, he could not obey because of mitigating circumstances.

At last, unable to continue a gentlemanly resistance to his uncle any longer, Manuel Salcedo formally resumed the gubernatorial office on Sunday, December 15, 1811.[119] Once again he faced the insurmountable task of safeguarding the province from internal and external pressures.

As before, the military problems consumed most of Salcedo's time. One piece of unfinished business, which doubtlessly touched off discomforting memories, related to José de Rossi, who reportedly was in Cuba doggedly trying to procure armaments for Texas.[120] Compared with Apolinar Masmela, who stayed close to home, Rossi had traveled far in the quest of his objective. To be sure, the eruption of the Las Casas revolt in Béxar had temporarily altered Masmela's plans, but even so he failed to show initiative. It was almost one year after Salcedo issued the first commission to him before Masmela finally departed for Louisiana. Because of the risk involved in crossing the Neutral Ground east of Nacogdoches, the governor had provided Masmela with as little money as possible. Instead, the procurement agent

---

[118] Vicente Travieso to Salcedo, Béxar, November 22, 1811, BA.

[119] Castañeda, *Our Catholic Heritage in Texas*, VI, 41.

[120] As late as March, 1812, Rossi was in Tampico, from where he reported to Salcedo that illness prevented him from shipping the military equipment to Texas (The Governor [of Texas] to Nemesio Salcedo, Béxar, November 27, 1811; Nemesio Salcedo to Governor of Texas [Salcedo], Chihuahua, April 27, 1812, BA).

took a string of mules to exchange in Natchitoches for the war supplies needed in Spanish Texas.[121]

In other aspects of the defense question, Don Nemesio, with reference to furloughs for officers and enlisted men, reminded Salcedo of the obligation to maintain expenses at a minimum level so as to prevent a drain on the Real Hacienda.[122] Indeed, the commandant general showed very little understanding of frontier conditions in Texas. At the height of the years of crises, he failed to differentiate between words and weapons. In contrast, Salcedo the realist never deceived himself that the spirit of rebellion, which he and others had suppressed at the Wells of Baján, was spent. Be that as it may, having accepted the governorship for a second time, he determined to defend the province with his life if necessary. As the year 1811 closed, Don Manuel hardly suspected that he personified the end of an era.

---

[121] The Governor [of Texas] to Trudeaux, Béxar, December 15, 1811, BA.

[122] Nemesio Salcedo to Governor of Texas [Salcedo], Chihuahua, December 10, 1811, BA.

6. THE COLLAPSE OF
SALCEDO'S RULE

MANUEL MARÍA DE SALCEDO began the new year of 1812 with firm resolve. The disagreement with the commandant general had strained the correct relationship between the two strong-willed men, but all the same Salcedo persevered in his duties as governor. With a scarcity of matériel and manpower, he struggled to defend Spanish Texas' tottering defenses. Royalism, despite bureaucratic shortsightedness, was a way of life to which Salcedo the cavalier instinctively responded. After three long years of frontier service, he sensed the danger of revolutionary ideas—independence and its ramifications—that threatened the integrity of the loyalist structure. In vain, he repeatedly warned superior officials that the province was defenseless against ideological subversion. Almost alone, he faced the inevitable collapse.

Early in January, 1812, Bernardo Montero, the commandant who replaced Cristóbal Domínguez at Nacogdoches, notified the Béxar authorities that Apolinar Masmela, the governor's purchasing agent, had arrived in East Texas, where he sought respite due to the uncertainty of safe passage through the Neutral Ground.[1] While the procurement representative waited for a favorable time in which to continue his trip to Natchitoches, Governor Salcedo in Béxar reassessed the deplorable fiscal conditions of his administration and asked Don Nemesio for eight thousand pesos to stabilize the provincial treasury.[2]

The deteriorated condition of the East Texas line of defense, undoubtedly complicated by a resurgence of banditry in the Neutral Zone, prompted Hispanic guardians to readjust their troop deployments. On orders from Salcedo, Montero transferred fifty cavalrymen from the Nacogdoches garrison to the Trinidad outpost.[3] Montero failed to tell the governor, however, that the men lacked horses; the Trinidad commander quickly complained to Don Manuel, adding further that he also needed flour and money.[4] Meanwhile Apolinar Masmela, warned by Spanish Vice-Consul Félix Trudeaux about lawlessness along the road to Natchitoches, waited in Nacogdoches for the governor to send further instructions.[5] The commandant general, emphasizing prudent management in financial matters, directed Salcedo to postpone paying the presidial troops until economic conditions improved. A subsequent retrenchment measure called for demobilization of the colonial militia whenever the Indian menace subsided.[6]

As a matter of fact, the eruption of Indian hostilities in 1812

---

[1] Bernardo Montero to Herrera, Nacogdoches, January 3, 1812, Béxar Archives, Eugene C. Barker Texas History Center, The University of Texas at Austin. Herinafter cited as BA.

[2] Salcedo to Nemesio Salcedo, Béxar, January 8, 1812, BA.

[3] Montero to Salcedo, Nacogdoches, January 3, 1812, BA.

[4] Felipe de la Garza to Salcedo, Trinidad, January 13, 1812, B.A.

[5] Montero to Salcedo, Nacogdoches, January 13, 1812, BA.

[6] Nemesio Salcedo to Governor of Texas [Salcedo], Chihuahua, January 18, 21, 1812, BA.

was one problem over which Hispanic Texans exercised little control and which made it expedient to keep the militia in operation. Frequently native marauders attacked small mounted patrols,[7] but quite often Spanish troops bravely repelled the thrusts.[8]

During these troubled days, Governor Salcedo kept track of the welfare of his wife and infant daughter in New Orleans through the Hispanicized Irish trader in Nacogdoches, Samuel Davenport, whose own wife was seriously ill, a personal concern that he shared with Don Manuel.[9] Fortified with the knowledge that his family was safe, Salcedo grimly faced material shortages in Béxar. A supplier in Monterrey notified the governor that he could not furnish the paper and clothing Béxar residents desperately needed, because his stock was temporarily depleted. Nonetheless, the merchant held out the hope that as soo as an expected shipment arrived from Veracruz he would advise the Texas executive.[10] In fact, stamped paper became so scarce that Montero of Nacogdoches lent sixty sheets to the Trinidad commander, pledging to convey more when he received a full ream himself![11] During this crisis a few soldiers, such as the commander of the San Marcos settlement, volunteered to augment the cavalry herds by rounding up wild horses, but the governor, although he sympathized with their initiative, disapproved the plan because of the danger involved to men and mounts. To maintain morale, however, he offered to consider permitting the troops to search for runaway branded horses among the mustangs.[12] The hard-

[7] Salcedo to Commandant General [Nemesio Salcedo], Béxar, January 22, 1812; Diary of Juan Caso, Béxar, January 24, 1812, BA.

[8] Mariano Rodríguez to Salcedo, Béxar, January 24, 1812, BA.

[9] Samuel Davenport to Salcedo, Nacogdoches, January 23, 1812, February 14, 1812, BA.

[10] José María de Sada to Salcedo, Monterrey, January 30, 1812, BA.

[11] Montero to Salcedo, Nacogdoches, February 3, 1812, BA.

[12] Salcedo to Commander of San Marcos, Béxar, February 4, 1812, BA.

ships endured by Hispanic Texans in the winter months of 1812 are evident from a gubernatorial report to Don Nemesio, in which Salcedo bitterly complained not only of a shortage of firewood for heating purposes by the soldiers on sentry duty, but also of the lack of candles for illuminating the guardhouse and the military barracks.[13]

Evidently another aspect of colonial administration that plagued Salcedo pertained to corporal punishment. The commandant general replied to an inquiry by the governor that imperial law prohibited torture, including whipping, as a penal method.[14] Salcedo may have asked for a clarification of a disciplinary technique practiced on uncooperative Indians by the mission guards, but, in view of recent difficulties, it is also entirely possible that he contemplated applying the lash to recalcitrant rebels of lower rank. However, on learning of the royal prohibition on whipping, he declared his obedience to the law.[15]

Tension continued to mount on the Texas-Louisiana frontier. Davenport notified Salcedo that outlaws again were active in the Neutral Zone.[16] Captain Montero reported that bandits had attacked a courier, but the Spaniard, displaying great presence of mind, had destroyed the letters he carried before being captured. Thus thwarted, the highwaymen had merely robbed the messenger of a few chattels.[17] Despite this overt provocation to Spanish arms, Montero was powerless to retaliate beyond the west bank of the Sabine River. Most of his troops, he told the governor, were without cavalry mounts and many of them lacked shoes. Even so, Montero assigned a detachment at the river's edge to prevent

[13] Nemesio Salcedo to Governor of Texas [Salcedo], Chihuahua, February 4, 1812, BA.

[14] Salcedo to Commandant General [Nemesio Salcedo], Béxar, March 18, 1812, BA.

[15] Salcedo to Commandant General [Nemesio Salcedo], Béxar, February 5, 1812, BA.

[16] Davenport to Salcedo, Nacogdoches, February 6, 1812, BA.

[17] Montero to Salcedo, Nacogdoches, February 14, 1812, BA.

Neutral Ground raiders from entering Hispanic territory. Partially to correct a deplorable situation, the Nacogdoches commander requisitioned flour and other supplies for the commissary and
asked for mules to reinforce the mail service.[18]

While Montero's plea for assistance was en route to Béxar,
Apolinar Masmela, in the company of a sizable party traveling
to Natchitoches, crossed the Neutral Ground. As the group approached a creek identified as Arroyo de la Nana an outlaw gang,
about twelve in number, assaulted the travelers, killing one and
wounding three others. This time the marauders fled when Masmela's companions, principally the military guards, repelled the
attack. After arriving in Natchitoches, the procurement agent
reported the incident to the Texas governor.[19] It was now obvious
that the lawless element in the Neutral Zone so endangered
frontiersmen on both sides of the Sabine River that neither the
United States nor New Spain could continue ignoring the outlaws' presence.

In Béxar, Governor Salcedo and Colonel Herrera reviewed the
defense question as it affected the center and the perimeter of
the province. On February 15, Don Manuel appointed a military
council on public safety with jurisdiction over cases of sedition.[20]
Within a week the special board held its first session, to hear the
charges against a former royalist officer, José Menchaca, who
reportedly had instigated an abortive insurrection in San Antonio. After the council rendered a guilty verdict, Governor
Salcedo dispatched the accused under protective custody to Don
Nemesio in Chihuahua.[21]

---

[18] Montero to Salcedo, Nacogdoches, Letters 42 and 44, February 18,
1812, BA.
   [19] Apolinar Masmela to Salcedo, Natchitoches, February 26, 1812; Montero
to Salcedo, Nacogdoches, April 2, 1812, BA.
   [20] Salcedo to Herrera, Béxar, February 15, 1812, BA.
   [21] Salcedo to Cordero and Nemesio Salcedo, Béxar, February 20–March 8,
1812, BA.

In the meantime, Hispanic guardians in Texas learned of the devious activities of José Antonio Álvarez de Toledo, a Cuban adventurer in search of lucrative intrigues. Salcedo immediately issued a warrant for Álvarez de Toledo's arrest.[22] Next, Don Manuel clamped down on foreign residents who had arrived in Béxar after September, 1810, presumably from other Spanish settlements in Texas, by ordering them to leave the capital within three days. Apparently the alcaldes, responsible for carrying out the governor's mandate, found it difficult to meet the deadline; on the third day Don Manuel rebuked two of them for negligence.[23]

Actually Salcedo's policy vis-à-vis foreigners was one of control, not persecution. He informed his uncle of secret orders sent to the Nacogdoches commander to arrest all interlopers who did not have the benefit of proper credentials.[24] By inference, the governor intended to respect alien settlers who complied with Spanish colonial law in their pursuit of honest livelihoods.

Turning to purely military affairs, the Texas governor requested special permission to restructure the royal forces in Texas. Normally it required forty-six days for a piece of correspondence to be processed from Béxar to Chihuahua and back. To overcome this handicap, Salcedo asked Don Nemesio to grant him discretionary power in discharging disabled troops and un-

[22] Clemente Delgado and Francisco Travieso to Salcedo, Béxar, February 25, 1812; Salcedo to Commandant General [Nemesio Salcedo], Béxar, March 4, 1812, BA. Álvarez de Toledo's activities are carefully traced in Philip C. Brooks, "Spain's Farewell to Louisiana, 1803–1821," *Mississippi Valley Historical Review*, 27, no. 1 (June, 1940), 29–42, and Harris Gaylord Warren, "José Álvarez de Toledo's Initiation as a Filibuster, 1811–1813," *Hispanic American Historical Review*, 20, no. 1 (February, 1940), 58–82.

[23] Salcedo to the People of Béxar, Béxar, February 26 [?], 1812; The Governor [Salcedo] to the Alcaldes of the First and Second Vote [District], Béxar, February 28, 1812, BA.

[24] Salcedo to Commandant General [Nemesio Salcedo], Béxar, Letter 59, March 4, 1812, BA.

desirable elements from the ranks.[25] Commendable as Don Manuel's plan for improving army administration appeared, Don Nemesio remained unmoved. Not only did he reprimand Salcedo for granting furloughs to officers and enlisted personnel without obtaining prior consent from the Chihuahua headquarters, but he also caustically reminded the governor that the prerogative of allowing or disallowing applications for separation from active service resided exclusively with the commandant general.[26]

If Don Manuel took personal delight in annoying his uncle, he found the ideal occasion when Ignacio Pérez, a captain attached to the Béxar garrison, filed a petition for eighteen months' overdue rent owed to him by one of Don Nemesio's favorite officers, Bernardo Bonavía, for the period when the former deputy commandant general lived in Texas. Salcedo judged the monthly rent of twenty-five pesos inadequate, considering how the cost of living had risen.[27] Responding to the insult, Don Nemesio displayed a wry sense of humor. Aside from acknowledging the government's debt, he deftly parried the governor's barb by ordering the Texas provincial treasury to honor Captain Pérez' claim in full![28]

Evidently by informal agreement among friends, Governor

---

[25] Salcedo to Commandant General [Nemesio Salcedo], Béxar, Letter 61, March 4, 1812, BA.

[26] Nemesio Salcedo to Governor of Texas [Salcedo], Chihuahua, February 29, 1812, BA.

[27] Salcedo to Commandant General [Nemesio Salcedo], Béxar, Letter 66, March 4, 1812, BA.

[28] Nemesio Salcedo to Governor of Texas [Salcedo], Chihuahua, April 13, 1812, BA. Five months later, the commandant general, obviously rankled by Salcedo's audacity in bringing up the unpleasant discussion of Bonavía's personal debts, informed Don Bernardo of the incident. Undoubtedly embarrassed, Bonavía asked the commandant general to determine the exact amount of his indebtedness in San Antonio de Béxar. Apart from this inquiry, the case ended in silence (Nemesio Salcedo to Governor of Texas [Salcedo], Chihuahua, August 4, 20, 1812, BA).

Salcedo, although a lieutenant colonel, shared his military authority with Simón de Herrera, who outranked him by one grade. However, Don Manuel's subordinates at the several outposts unquestionably understood that final responsibility in Texas rested with the political and military governor. Faced with the elusive task of Texas' eastern defenses, Governor Salcedo warned Captain Montero of Nacogdoches not to permit Spanish officers to exchange correspondence with their United States counterparts in Louisiana. Since Montero was new at this assignment, the governor merely reminded him that previous mandates on this subject were still applicable, a point about which Salcedo notified Colonel Herrera.[29]

The prohibition on communication did not apply to the gubernatorial office. From Natchitoches, Lieutenant Colonel Zebulon M. Pike, who had first-hand experiences in the Spanish borderlands, informed Montero that he had received orders to send a punitive expedition into the Neutral Ground to expel troublesome freebooters. Almost immediately the Nacogdoches captain dispatched a courier to Béxar with the latest information, including Pike's request for cooperation from Spanish troops as in the mutual expedition of 1810.[30] Governor Salcedo, unlike his uncle, promptly gave his approval and instructed Montero to detail one officer and twenty men, all neatly attired and well equipped, for the special mission. For the job of interpreter, Don Manuel earnestly recommended the services of Samuel Davenport.[31]

To dramatize the military urgency in Texas, Governor Salcedo ignored protocol and wrote directly to the viceroy of New Spain

[29] Salcedo to Commander of Nacogdoches [Montero], Béxar, March 5, 1812, BA.

[30] Zebulon M. Pike to Montero, Natchitoches, February 26, 1812; Montero to Governor of Texas [Salcedo], Nacogdoches, February 29, 1812, BA.

[31] Salcedo to Commander of Nacogdoches [Montero], Béxar, March 12, 1812, BA.

about troop strength in the province, a figure Herrera had set at
1,136. He included copies of relevant documents he had sent to
Don Nemesio. Salcedo's experience on the frontier had made him
cognizant of the virtual independence that existed between Chihuahua and Mexico City, but he also recognized that imperial
emergencies, not excluding Indian depredations, tended to blur
lines of authority. Since Texas was the gateway to New Spain
from the northern borderlands, as governor he had the duty to
tap all possible sources of assistance for its defense.[32] Shortly
thereafter, Cordero of Coahuila, who certainly was in a position
to know, apprised Salcedo that six thousand royalist troops had
reportedly disembarked in Veracruz and an additional two thousand were expected. Even with partial reinforcements from these
new contingents, Cordero, expressing the hope that the Comanche
raiders could be chastised, promised to aid his fellow royalists in
Texas by transferring parts of his command north of the Rio
Grande.[33] This time he kept his word. An officer stationed on the
periphery of the province of Coahuila, Cristóbal Domínguez of
the Presidio del Rio Grande, hurriedly dispatched forty men on
a forced march to Béxar.[34]

In these trying days, Salcedo definitely needed support, especially in the mail service. Captain Montero, still waiting for the
horses or mules he had requisitioned, declared to the governor
that on the average it took the mail sixteen days to get from
Béxar to Nacogdoches, often because the couriers were on foot.[35]
One piece of news that eventually did reach Nacogdoches pertained to the expedition into the Neutral Ground. Montero
quickly notified Pike of Salcedo's willingness to cooperate in the

---

[32] Salcedo to the Viceroy of New Spain, Béxar, March 10, 1812, BA.
[33] Cordero to Salcedo, Monclova, March 16, 1812, BA.
[34] Domínguez to Salcedo, Presidio del Rio Grande, March 21, 1812, BA.
[35] Montero to Salcedo, Nacogdoches, March 17, 1812, BA.

joint effort to exterminate the outlaws.[36] Don Nemesio, who remembered Pike from an earlier occasion, had permitted the
Texas governor to proceed according to plan, but he had cautioned Don Manuel to be prepared to repel aggression.[37]

But, as the Spaniards in East Texas outfitted themselves and
looked for sturdy mounts, Zebulon Pike grew impatient with
Hispanic indecision. Finally, on March 5, he ordered two officers and forty men to invade the Neutral Zone, where they destroyed all habitats—houses, tents, hideouts, and encampments.
Besides apprehending sixteen men, the United States troops
rounded up thirty-five horses and mules and confiscated "many
bundles of merchandise, arms, and ammunition." Afterward,
Captain W. H. Overton, commandant at Natchitoches, informed
Montero that the Anglo-American success made a Spanish expedition unnecessary.[38]

To the Hispanic mind, the unilateral invasion of the Neutral
Ground by the United States army constituted a serious affront
to imperial honor. When Montero wrote to Salcedo on April 1
about the Anglo-American action, he declared his intention to
send a detail across the Sabine. Obviously, the Nacogdoches commander chose to ignore Captain Overton's suggestion. All the
same, before ordering Spanish troops eastward, Montero re-
luctantly admitted that necessity compelled him to borrow horses
from the local settlers, with a pledge to replace the animals if the
soldiers lost them on the campaign.[39]

Thirteen days later Captain Montero informed Governor Salcedo that Captain Isidro de la Garza—leading a contingent of one

[36] Montero to Pike, Nacogdoches, March 23, 1812, BA.

[37] Nemesio Salcedo to Governor of Texas [Salcedo], Chihuahua, March 26,
1812, BA.

[38] J. Villasana Haggard, "The Neutral Ground between Louisiana and
Texas, 1806–1821," *Louisiana Historical Quarterly*, 28, no. 4 (October, 1945),
1067.

[39] Montero to Salcedo, Nacogdoches, Letters 84 and 86, April 1, 1812, BA.

sergeant, two corporals, and seventeen privates—had penetrated
the Neutral Ground.[40] Hampered by heavy downpours, Captain
De la Garza slowly proceeded into the disputed territory; he encountered only "the charred remains" of the places formerly occupied by outlaws. On April 21, Don Isidro returned to Texas
without having captured a single bandit,[41] but his presence in the
Neutral Zone doubtlessly restored honor to the Spanish code of
arms. Subsequently, by reason of extreme hardships, Captain
Montero withdrew the detachment assigned to guard the west
bank of the Sabine River. He assured the governor, however, that
mounted patrols would periodically inspect the terrain to ferret
out smugglers and traitorous Spaniards.[42]

   Against the background of Hispanic awareness of renewed tension along the eastern border, royalist reaction in Nacogdoches,
San Antonio de Béxar, Monclova, and Chihuahua is understandable. Salcedo's plan for reorganizing the loyalist troops was one
manifestation of the anxiety. Another was Don Nemesio's complaint about the frequency of furloughs taken by soldiers in
Texas. Certainly the Coahuilan governor's sending of reinforcements, albeit minimal, fitted the general pattern of readjustment.
Finally, the willingness of Salcedo and others to cooperate with
the Anglo-American military in clearing the Neutral Ground of
banditti, however tardily executed, was a further sign of Spanish
apprehension.

   Despite the momentary pacification of the Neutral Ground by
United States soldiers, Hispanic officials continued to worry about
the Texas-Louisiana frontier. As the bleak winter days gave way
to the spring season, the area between the Arroyo Hondo and
the Sabine River again teemed with adventurous souls—leaders
of consequence, followers of obscure causes, and ne'er-do-wells—

[40] Montero to Salcedo, Nacogdoches, April 14, 1812, BA.
[41] Haggard, "The Neutral Ground between Louisiana and Texas," p. 1068.
[42] Montero to Salcedo, Nacogdoches, April 29, 1812, BA.

who incessantly watched the border for the first auspicious opportunity to foment unrest in New Spain.

Before the invasion of the Neutral Ground, Salcedo's procurement agent Masmela had written from Natchitoches that, because supplies were not available in upper Louisiana, he planned to go to New Orleans. To expedite the trip, he decided to leave his mules at the Red River settlement, probably in the custody of the Spanish vice-consul, so as to enhance their value.[43] Two days after Masmela left Natchitoches for New Orleans, Félix Trudeaux advised Salcedo to send to the Red River a herd of additional mules, preferably two hundred to three hundred head, to improve Don Apolinar's bargaining position amid adverse trading conditions. Moreover, the vice-consul advised Don Manuel to provide Masmela with a large amount of cash, to impress Louisiana merchants that the Hispanic government of Texas deserved to be trusted.[44]

A gesture of governmental concern about Masmela's mission was a communiqué from Salcedo to Spanish consul Diego Murphy in New Orleans, reporting that Matagorda Bay on the coast of Texas had been declared an open port by the king. This was obviously a suggestion for Murphy to advise Don Apolinar to use that facility. More important in terms of imperial security was Don Manuel's comment in the same letter on the menace to legitimacy posed by the activities of an upstart rebel leader, Bernardo Gutiérrez de Lara.[45] This was a clear indication that Hispanic authorities were constantly aware of movements, however minimal, that threatened the borderlands. Unlike lesser disturbances, however, Gutiérrez' agitation, when unleashed, was to destroy irreparably the inner fiber of royalism in Texas.

Shortly before the rebel Hidalgo forces were defeated at the

---

[43] Masmela to Salcedo, Natchitoches, March 21, 1812, BA.
[44] Trudeaux to Salcedo, Natchitoches, March 23, 1812, BA.
[45] Salcedo to Murphy, Béxar, April 21, 1812, BA.

Wells of Baján in March, 1811, Bernardo Gutiérrez unreservedly
committed himself to the cause of Mexican independence. In addition to a lieutenant colonelcy, he received a commission to seek
material support from the United States. Convinced of the righteousness of his ideals, Gutiérrez, accompanied by an acquaint-
ance from Béxar, set out from his hometown of Revilla. Circum-
venting the Camino Real to avoid passing near loyalist outposts,
the Mexican envoy and his companion proceeded eastward until,
close to Nacogdoches, an alert patrol detected their presence in
the vicinity and hurriedly chased them into the piney woods of
East Texas. There the fugitives eluded their pursuers. Crossing
the Sabine River, Gutiérrez found unexpected refuge among
Neutral Ground inhabitants, who quickly conveyed the news of
his arrival to interested border observers in Natchitoches, hotbed
of frontier intrigue. At the Red River entrepôt, in October, 1811,
Anglo-American authorities, civilian and military, eagerly provided the means by which the diplomat from Revilla continued
the journey to Washington, D.C. When Colonel Gutiérrez arrived at the United States capital in December, he lost little time
in discussing the object of his mission with James Monroe, secretary of state in the Madison administration, who unofficially
sympathized with the Mexican independence movement. Owing
to Gutiérrez' unorthodox diplomatic status and Monroe's overt
expansionist views, however, the conversations ended in failure.
All the same, Gutiérrez, with assistance from the State Department, acquired a social and political acumen that enabled him to
meet a number of temporary residents in Washington. Among
these was Álvarez de Toledo, the Caribbean soldier of fortune
for whose arrest Governor Salcedo had issued a warrant.[46] One

---

[46] Vidal Covián Martínez, *Don José Bernardo Maximiliano Gutiérrez de
Lara*, pp. 6–9. For a sympathetic, scholarly study of Bernardo Gutiérrez, see
Julia Kathryn Garrett, *Green Flag over Texas: A Story of the Last Years of
Spain in Texas*. A romanticized, yet valuable, account of Gutiérrez' filibuster-

important personage with whom Gutiérrez did not fraternize was Luis de Onís, unaccredited Spanish diplomat to the United States, who regularly apprised Texas authorities of any activity, particularly Gutiérrez', that he deemed detrimental to his sovereign's imperial holdings in North America.[47]

In January, 1812, Bernardo Gutiérrez, having accomplished nothing of substance, left Washington for Baltimore and Philadelphia, stopping long enough in the latter city to enlist the pamphleteering services of Álvarez de Toledo, who agreed to work behind the scenes to overthrow royalist rule in Texas. By early March, Colonel Gutiérrez, again in Louisiana, encountered United States special agent William Shaler, who encouraged him in fomenting revolutionary aggression.[48]

Firebrand Gutiérrez' return to the frontier generated much interest, for different reasons, in several quarters of Louisiana. At the end of April, Diego Murphy warned Montero of Nacogdoches of the arrival from Philadelphia of a suspicious character who claimed to be a colonel of the Mexican insurgents.[49] Obviously the Spanish consul referred to Colonel Gutiérrez. About a week

---

ing activities from the outbreak of the Hidalgo revolt to the initial years of Mexican nationhood is Rie Jarratt, *Gutiérrez de Lara, Mexican-Texan: The Story of a Creole Hero.*

[47] Luis de Onís to Salcedo, Washington, D.C., December 21, 1811; cited in Salcedo to Onís, Béxar, May 19, 1812, BA.

[48] Covián Martínez, *Don José Bernardo Maximiliano Gutiérrez de Lara,* p. 11. William Shaler, of Bridgeport, Connecticut, spent the first decade of the nineteenth century as a sea captain in the Pacific, after which he published an account of his travels—"Journal of a Voyage Between China and Northwestern Coast of America"—in the *American Register* (1808). In January, 1812, in the service of the United States Department of State, Shaler transferred from Havana, Cuba, to Natchitoches, Louisiana, in order to obtain firsthand information on the filibustering activities in the Neutral Ground (Webb [ed.], *Handbook of Texas,* II, 596).

[49] Morphy [*sic*] to Commander of Nacogdoches [Montero], New Orleans, April 26, 1812, BA.

later, Félix Trudeaux sent the following message to the Nacogdoches commandant: "Bernardo Gutiérrez has returned here
[Natchitoches] from the United States and with him is an Amer-
can who seems to be of much importance. It is reported that his
[Gutiérrez'] intentions are to seek every means to revolutionize
the Internal Provinces."[50] At this critical juncture, Montero received a food and money shipment from Governor Salcedo. The
one thousand pesos he immediately used to pay the enlisted personnel who heretofore had received script in lieu of currency.[51]

Coincidental with Gutiérrez' return to the Texas-Louisiana
frontier, Hispanic guardians in San Antonio reassembled imperial defenses. On March 28, the first detachment of veteran
troops sent by Cristóbal Domínguez of the Rio Grande presidio
arrived at the capital, led by Alférez Cadena, who promptly reported to Governor Salcedo. Don Manuel distributed the new-
comers among different units and reserved the next group of replacements, especially the least equipped, to escort the supply
master.[52] The Rio Grande veterans strengthened the defensive
perimeter around Béxar at a time when Indian marauders intensified their aggressive assaults. Ironically, as the situation
temporarily improved at the Texas center, it tended to deteriorate
along the Rio Grande to the west. Because of increased Indian
hostilities in the area under his jurisdiction, Domínguez seriously contemplated changing the mail schedule and, if necessary,
even ordering the total abandonment of the presidio itself.[53] To
provide some protection to the postal riders who traversed the
Béxar–Rio Grande road, Governor Salcedo promised Domínguez

50 Walter Flavius M'Caleb, "The First Period of the Gutierrez-Magee
Expedition," *Quarterly of the Texas State Historical Association*, 4, no. 3
(January, 1901), 220–221.
51 Montero to Salcedo, Nacogdoches, Letter 99, April 1, 1812, Letter 121,
April 28, 1812, BA.
52 Salcedo to Domínguez, Béxar, March 31, 1812, BA.
53 Domínguez to Salcedo, Presidio del Rio Grande, April 6, 1812, BA.

that he would again station a detachment at the Frio River. Since mounted patrols regularly policed the Indian trails, Don Manuel recommended keeping the current timetable for the mail run.[54] Shortly thereafter, another Rio Grande detachment of mostly volunteers and lancers arrived in Béxar and placed their services at Salcedo's disposal.[55]

With the additional manpower, the Texas governor, for the time being, pacified the area between Béxar and the Rio Grande. He sent out a 665-man punitive expedition, which succeeded in forcing the Indians to accept peaceful coexistence. Subinspector Domínguez unabashedly rejoiced at the sight of Spanish troops in pursuit of fleeing natives. After Salcedo's reoccupation of the Frio River outpost, Don Cristóbal indicated that he would continue sending the mail to that location.[56]

As far as possible, Hispanics in Texas, with welcomed assistance from Coahuila, restructured their defenses. Loyalists in the lower Rio Grande settlements of Mier and Camargo fared less successfully. At Camargo, Pedro López Prietto, former garrison leader at Trinidad, resisted an Indian attack until the aggressors, undoubtedly with rebel support, overpowered him and other prominent citizens. From Laredo, Governor Salcedo received an appeal for aid.[57] Unable to send troops without weakening his own position, Don Manuel used the only practical option open to him and asked Lieutenant Colonel Díaz de Bustamante of Laredo to go downriver and break the siege on Camargo. Upriver, Cristóbal Domínguez, in his capacity as subinspector of troops, quickly dispatched Lieutenant Colonel Ignacio Elizondo to assist in the campaign. In fact, Don Cristóbal, before he knew for certain that Camargo had been liberated, assembled a force

---

[54] Salcedo to Domínguez, Béxar, April 11, 1812, BA.
[55] Félix de Cevallos to Salcedo, Béxar, April 12, 1812, BA.
[56] Domínguez to Salcedo, Presidio del Rio Grande, April 15, 29, 1812, BA.
[57] José Antonio Benavides to Salcedo, Laredo, April 11, 1812, BA.

of 150 men to reinforce the royalist troops in the lower Rio Grande.[58]

After scattering the rebels at Camargo, Díaz de Bustamante courteously notified Salcedo that Colonel Joaqúin de Arredondo, commander of the viceregal forces in the provinces adjacent to south Texas, had requested him to take charge of the governor-ship of Nuevo León.[59] Although the counterinsurgency move-ments had occurred outside the Texas boundaries, Governor Sal-cedo grasped the significance of the events. He knew that any realignment of Spanish troops south of the Rio Grande would definitely weaken royalist defenses in Texas, particularly in the Sabine River area.

Indian raids east of the Texas capital constantly plagued His-panic guardians. Governor Salcedo severely reprimanded the post commander at the San Marcos River for allowing a wander-ing band of Indians to slaughter cattle in his vicinity.[60] Farther east, at Villa Trinidad, Captain Felipe de la Garza informed the governor of the alarming number of problems that beset him, all of which touched on the Indian menace. First, the mail couriers had been attacked and the service briefly interrupted. One of the carriers, critically wounded, managed to reach the Trinity out-post, where he received succor. A rescue party that rode out after the Indians found two other couriers and recovered some of the scattered mail. Captain De la Garza assigned a sergeant, in charge of seven privates, to escort the messengers in the future. Second, owing to limited munitions and anticipated hostilities, the commander planned to construct a palisade for the protection of settlers and soldiers. Finally, to top his troubles, Captain De la Garza had arrested the Indian interpreter, Asencio Arriola, who ostensibly had stirred up discontent among the natives. Not want-

[58] Domínguez to Salcedo, Presidio del Rio Grande, April 29, 1812, BA.
[59] Díaz de Bustamente to Salcedo, Camargo, April 30, 1812, BA.
[60] Salcedo to Commander at San Marcos, Béxar, May 1, 1812, BA.

ing to keep Arriola lodged in the Trinidad guardhouse, Don Felipe asked Salcedo to remove the prisoner and to appoint another interpreter.[61]

Within a short period, the Trinidad commander appealed to Governor Salcedo for relief. Besides the usual military supplies and personnel he needed, he petitioned Don Manuel for authority to recall Trinidad soldiers on detached duty to other outposts. Don Felipe found himself in such a dire circumstance that he asked for a blacksmith from Atascosito to repair unserviceable weapons. More deplorable, however, was the destruction of the military quarters and guardhouse by a severe wind-and-rain storm. In desperation Captain De la Garza assigned Corporal Góngora, equipped with an ax, to erect a defensive wall. If these complications were not enough, Don Felipe, now without a jail, still had to contend with the problem of detaining the insubordinate Indian interpreter.[62] Eventually the embarrassing question of the translator resolved itself. The Trinidad captain conducted an interrogation, in the presence of reliable officers; a witness, hidden in an adjoining room, later verified the authenticity of Arriola's translations. Apparently satisfied with the Indian interpreter's loyalty, Don Felipe released the prisoner. When the outpost commander notified Governor Salcedo of the proceedings, he also announced the completion of the stockade he had planned.[63] Tardily and ineffectively, the commandant general, demonstrating how distance prejudiced his views on Texas, told Salcedo that the Trinidad fort should be abandoned and the troops merged with the Béxar forces.[64]

[61] Felipe de la Garza to Salcedo, Trinidad, Letters 98, 99, 100, and 101, May 2, 1812, BA.

[62] Felipe de la Garza to Salcedo, Trinidad, Letters 104, 106, 107, and 108, May 10, 1812, BA.

[63] Felipe de la Garza to Salcedo, Trinidad, Letters 111 and 112, June 1, 1812, BA.

[64] Nemesio Salcedo to Salcedo, Chihuahua, June 9, 1812, BA.

From the provincial capital, Manuel de Salcedo again wrote
to the viceroy of New Spain about the recent successful campaigns along the lower Rio Grande, in which some troops stationed on the periphery of Texas had played a significant role.
Keenly aware, however, that any redeployment of soldiers away
from the borders of Texas was detrimental to the overall defensive posture, the governor asked that Díaz de Bustamante be retained at the Laredo presidio and that a coast guard vessel be
anchored at Matagorda Bay and another at Soto la Marina, far
to the south of the Rio Grande. Finally, Salcedo apprised the
viceregal office that he knew of Bernardo Gutiérrez' threat to
royalist stability.[65]

In East Texas, Bernardo Montero maintained a shaky position. The outpost he commanded was undermanned and badly
equipped. Salcedo, Herrera, and Montero were fully informed
of this deficiency. Yet the Nacogdoches captain wondered how
much support he could expect from the civilian populace in the
event of aggression. In the second week in May, 1812, he wrote
Salcedo that he had alerted the various commanders in the area
to seize all seditious literature that the rebel Gutiérrez undoubtedly would attempt to introduce into the borderlands.[66] Usually
the writer of unpleasant tidings, Montero notified the governor
that Indians had wounded three enlisted men who conveyed the
mail to Nacogdoches, causing them to lose part of the dispatches.
Unable to retrieve the missing letters, the captain asked Salcedo
to rewrite the correspondence![67]

Woefully surrounded with administrative details, most of
which focused on the East Texas question, Don Manuel announced to the townspeople of Béxar that their local government
was concerned with their welfare and invited them to participate

[65] Salcedo to the Viceroy of New Spain, Béxar, May 11, 1812, BA.
[66] Montero to Salcedo, Nacogdoches, Letter 126, May 12, 1812, BA.
[67] Montero to Salcedo, Nacogdoches, Letter 128, May 13, 1812, BA.

in the election of trusted individuals to serve on the municipal council. Most urgently, he appealed to the citizenry to support the system by willingly paying their tax obligations.[68]

For the moment, the management of capital affairs appeared under control. More immediately pressing was finding a way of safeguarding the eastern border. To this end, Governor Salcedo directed the commander at the San Marcos River settlement to provide a ten-man guard to protect the mail riders as they traversed the royal road to Nacogdoches.[69] Finally, after considerable delay, Salcedo prepared to send twelve thousand pesos, some of which were for Apolinar Masmela's use in purchasing supplies, to Captain Montero. The governor also filled a backlog of requisitions—principally horses, flour, and small equipment—for the Nacogdoches garrison.[70]

In other aspects of colonial administration, the Texas executive seldom missed an opportunity to express his opinion. With reference to Díaz de Bustamante's tentative appointment as governor of Nuevo León, Don Manuel informed the viceroy that, although the former commandant of the Laredo presidio was quite capable of extinguishing pockets of rebellion around Camargo, he was untrained to assume such an important responsibility as a gubernatorial office.[71] From Salcedo's standpoint, Díaz de Bustamante's promotion, complicated by the danger of insurrection in the lower Rio Grande Valley, appeared to be dictated from Mexico City and not from Chihuahua. Accordingly, Don Manuel felt compelled to explain how administrative changes in provinces bordering Texas indirectly affected his own position. In this

---

[68] Salcedo to the Townspeople of Béxar, May 18, 1812, BA.

[69] Salcedo to Commanders at San Marcos, Trinidad, and Nacogdoches, Béxar, May 20, 1812, BA.

[70] Salcedo to Commander at Nacogdoches [Montero], Béxar, May 27, 1812, BA.

[71] Salcedo to the Viceroy of New Spain, Béxar, June 1, 1812, BA.

instance, loyalist Colonel Joaquín de Arredondo, commanding
the viceregal troops south of Nuevo León, seemed determined to
subordinate Díaz de Bustamante's appointment to the authority
of Mexico City.[72] Governor Salcedo, on the other hand, genuinely
worried about the unpredictable menace to Spanish Texas that
Bernardo Gutiérrez' presence in Louisiana signified, ordered
Díaz de Bustamante to release all Texas soldiers serving in Camargo and to send them back to Béxar.[73] Apologetically, the liberator of Camargo avowed to Salcedo that he had already advised
the viceregal office that the Texas governor's orders prevented
him from accepting the command of Nuevo León but that the
viceroy nonetheless had reiterated the mandate for Díaz de
Bustamante to remain at his present location to pacify the Indians.[74] The officer from Laredo realized that he stood midway
in a bureaucratic struggle. He soon extricated himself cleverly
from this uncomfortable position by communicating directly
with the commandant general of the Interior Provinces. When
Don Nemesio learned about the quagmire of words, not only did
he praise Díaz de Bustamante's work in suppressing rebellion in
the lower Río Grande area, but he also reprimanded the governor
of Texas for casting disparaging remarks about a fellow officer's
administrative capabilities.[75] Colonel Arredondo, taking advantage of his association with the Mexico City bureaucracy, informed Salcedo that the viceroy had designated Díaz de Bustamante as governor of Nuevo León and as ad interim governor of
Nuevo Santander. Pending formal installation to office, however,
Don Joaquín directed the Laredo frontiersman to pacify the Río

    [72] Joaquín de Arredondo to Salcedo, Quartel General del Valle de Maíz,
June 1, 1812, BA.
    [73] Salcedo to Díaz de Bustamante, Béxar, June 1, 1812, BA.
    [74] Díaz de Bustamante to Salcedo, Camargo, June 16, 1812, BA.
    [75] Nemesio Salcedo to the Governor of Texas [Salcedo], Chihuahua, June
19, 1812, BA.

Grande villas.[76] Undaunted by these developments, Manuel Salcedo pressed his claim to the Texas contingent; finally the defender of Camargo agreed to return fifty presidiaries to Béxar.[77]

As this dispute occupied the attention of Hispanic borderlanders, Bernardo Gutiérrez planned an invasion on the eastern threshold of Texas. At Natchitoches the rebel leader from Revilla obtained the professional services of a former lieutenant of the United States Army, Augustus William Magee, who assumed actual management of the filibustering expedition.[78] Another guiding figure who participated in the initial phases of the planning was William Shaler. In fact, according to one of Governor Salcedo's informants in Natchitoches, the United States agent's open fellowship with Gutiérrez undoubtedly influenced many frontiersmen to accept the Mexican firebrand as a duly accredited emissary.[79]

Without obstruction from military authorities in Louisiana, Gutiérrez and Magee advertised for armed supporters in the immediate environment as well as in Natchez and New Orleans. To enshroud their activities with the trappings of legality and thus encourage enlistments, the filibusters provided a name for the motley crew that assembled in the Neutral Ground—the Repub-

[76] Arredondo to Salcedo, Quartel General del Valle de Maíz, July 14, 1812, BA.

[77] Díaz de Bustamante to Salcedo, Camargo, August 6, 1812, BA.

[78] Lillian E. Fisher, "American Influence upon the Movement for Mexican Independence," *Mississippi Valley Historical Review*, 18, no. 4 (March, 1932), 470. Magee, a young Bostonian and graduate of the United States Military Academy, served on the Louisiana frontier under the command of General James Wilkinson from 1809 until his resignation from the army on June 22, 1812. When Magee assumed the leadership of Gutiérrez' soldiers-of-fortune, he was twenty-four years old (Harry McCorry Henderson, "The Magee-Gutierrez Expedition," *Southwestern Historical Quarterly*, 55, no. 1 [July, 1951], 43 n).

[79] Harris Gaylord Warren, *The Sword Was Their Passport: A History of American Filibustering in the Mexican Revolution*, p. 22.

lican Army of the North.[80] As the recruits slowly gathered in the territory over which no government exercised jurisdiction, Magee, a lieutenant colonel by the grace of Gutiérrez, undertook the military leadership of the planned invasion. Supposedly because of his ethnic background, he even furnished a green banner around which the Republican Army trained in the rudiments of warfare.[81] Gutiérrez, as nominal leader and symbol of the movement, concentrated on political questions, one of which involved propagandizing the Hispanic borderlands with the aim of nullifying opposition to the invaders.[82] Throughout the summer months of 1812, following the official outbreak of hostilities between the United States and Great Britain, the filibusters in the Neutral Zone enjoyed virtual immunity from arrest as they prepared to attack Spanish Texas.

West of the Sabine River, Governor Salcedo, aware of the danger building up day by day in Louisiana, grimly reassessed his vulnerable position. So concerned was Don Manuel about Gutiérrez' activities that in early June he informed the viceroy that he lacked troops he could trust.[83] Quite perplexing to Salcedo was his protracted struggle within the bureaucracy to clear himself of distrust, real or imagined, by superior leaders. Unable to get satisfaction from Don Nemesio, who perfunctorily thanked him in the name of the king for heroic and loyal services in 1811,[84] the Texas governor appealed to the viceroy for an examination of his case, claiming that one-time junior officers—ob-

---

[80] Henderson, "The Magee-Gutierrez Expedition," p. 45.

[81] M. L. Crimmins, "Augustus William Magee, the Second Advance Courier of American Expansion to Texas," *West Texas Historical Association Year Book*, 20 (October, 1944), 92.

[82] [Julia] Kathryn Garrett, "The First Newspaper of Texas: Gaceta de Texas," *Southwestern Historical Quarterly*, 40, no. 3 (January, 1937), 208.

[83] Salcedo to the Viceroy of New Spain, Béxar, June 2, 1812, BA.

[84] Nemesio Salcedo to Salcedo, Chihuahua, May 21, 1812, BA.

viously Herrera, Zambrano, and Díaz de Bustamante—now held appointments equal to his own, if not higher.[85]

Turning to more immediate needs, Don Manuel reported to his uncle that, according to the latest intelligence from the eastern border, Gutiérrez had been courteously received in the United States, where the rebel had obtained two printing presses to use in propagandizing the borderlands. Although Salcedo promised to protect Texas against Gutiérrez' insurgent designs, he disclosed that the means at his disposal were limited.[86] Curiously, the new emergency tended to reconcile the personal differences that existed among Béxar royalists. The governor informed Don Nemesio that one of the Zambrano brothers, José Darío, was an upstanding ecclesiastical leader.[87] In this instance, Don Manuel refrained from expressing his feelings toward another of the Zambranos, namely the subdeacon.

One clear indication of the seriousness of Bernardo Gutiérrez' revolutionary practices, the news of which assuredly distressed the Hispanics in the Texas capital, was the arrest of two rebel emissaries in Nacogdoches during the second week in June. Salcedo, when notified, promptly warned fellow royalists in Nuevo León, including Díaz de Bustamante, of the incident and avowed that the principal carrier would be shot in Béxar and his seditious papers burned.[88] Captain Montero of Nacogdoches lost little time in dispatching the confiscated propaganda to Governor Salcedo. Regrettably, the border guardian admitted that one rebel agent had escaped, but Montero swore that the fugitive would be appre-

---

[85] Salcedo to the Viceroy of New Spain, Béxar, June 3, 1812, BA.

[86] Salcedo to Commandant General [Nemesio Salcedo], Letter 139, Béxar, June 3, 1812, BA.

[87] Salcedo to Commandant General [Nemesio Salcedo], Letter 141, Béxar, June 3, 1812, BA.

[88] Salcedo to the Junta of Nuevo León, Governor of Colonia, [Díaz de] Bustamante, Béxar, June 8, 1812, BA.

hended the next time he approached the garrison wall with more literature.[89]

About the same time Apolinar Masmela, Salcedo's purchasing agent, temporarily returned to Nacogdoches. There he briefed Montero on his mission in Louisiana, made fruitless by an embargo imposed by the United States on exports. Significantly, he reported that, although the Anglo-American army had concentrated sizable forces near the international boundary, military leaders permitted outlaws to move freely into the Neutral Zone, where they augmented Gutiérrez' motley band of partisans.[90]

In Chihuahua Don Nemesio reacted in his usual fashion when he learned of insurgent activities in Louisiana. He ordered Governor Salcedo to seize all tracts that Gutiérrez' agents might scatter in the province. Furthermore, he urged his nephew to seek effective ways of capturing Gutiérrez and Álvarez de Toledo.[91] Without question, the commandant general expected his words to inspire confidence among Hispanics who, although stouthearted, lacked substantive reinforcements to ward off an imminent invasion.

Meanwhile the Nacogdoches commander woefully advised Salcedo that unless he obtained flour and corn by the end of June the garrison would be in dire straits.[92] The governor, who sincerely worried about the plight of his soldiers, shipped fourteen thousand pesos to sustain East Texas and to assist Masmela in purchasing supplies. The money caravan, led by Lieutenant Cantú, arrived in Nacogdoches on June 24, suffering only the

[89] Montero to Salcedo, Nacogdoches, June 8, 1812, BA.

[90] Masmela to Commander at Nacogdoches [Montero], Nacogdoches, June 9, 1812, BA.

[91] Nemesio Salcedo to Governor of Texas [Salcedo], Chihuahua, June 9, 1812, BA.

[92] Montero to Salcedo, Nacogdoches, June 11, 1812, BA.

loss of one horse, which drowned in the Trinity River.[93] For his part Captain Montero moved decisively at times. Late at night on June 27, after the mail courier had departed for Béxar, three of his men arrested José Francisco Venegas, a Gutiérrez agent, and seized the propaganda leaflets in his possession.[94] Shortly thereafter, Montero publicly burned Venegas' seditious papers and warned East Texas settlers and soldiers to follow the example or to suffer the consequences.[95]

In a desperate effort to restructure his defenses, Governor Salcedo directed Captain Isidro de la Garza, the officer who had penetrated the Neutral Ground, to assume command of the Trinidad outpost; he recalled Captain Felipe de la Garza to the capital.[96] Next, Salcedo implored the members of the Béxar garrison to uphold their honor as soldiers of the king and to imitate the valor of the East Texas sentries who had captured Gutiérrez' coinsurgents. To those soldiers who defended his capital, Salcedo bluntly declared that Venegas would be hanged as an object lesson to anyone who felt even the slightest temptation to distribute revolutionary proclamations.[97] Then, in a move to thwart the plans of propagandists in Natchitoches, Louisiana, Salcedo warned José María Peña, loyalist commandant at Revilla, that two Hispanic deserters, identified as Galván and Arispe, reportedly were on their way to spread seditious papers in the lower Rio Grande area.[98] In prompt reply to this warning, Peña

[93] Montero to Salcedo, Nacogdoches, June 24, 1812, BA.

[94] The alert sentries who captured Venegas were Alférez Encarnación Rodríguez, Corporal Ermenegildo [*sic*] Guillem, and Private Benito Martínez (Montero to Salcedo, Nacogdoches, June 27, 1812, BA).

[95] Montero to Salcedo, Nacogdoches, July 6, 1812, BA.

[96] Salcedo to Felipe de la Garza, Béxar, July 7, 1812; Salcedo to Ysidro de la Garza, Béxar, July 7, 1812, BA.

[97] Salcedo to the Troops of Béxar, Béxar, July 7, 1812, BA.

[98] Salcedo to José María Peña, Béxar, July 8, 1812, BA.

as well as Díaz de Bustamante assured the Texas governor that
patrols would be sent out to arrest the traitors if they managed to
get that far into the interior.[99]

In the midst of this crisis the commandant general was more
of a hindrance than anything else. As usual he reprimanded Governor Salcedo for writing complaints about deplorable conditions
in Texas. Moreover, Uncle Nemesio avowed that already he had
issued sufficient instructions to meet every circumstance that
might arise and further suggested to Don Manuel, probably as a
censorship ploy, the advisability of processing mail addressed to
the viceroy through Chihuahua, the most pacific of the northern
provinces. In fact, the commandant general soon upbraided Salcedo again, because the military reports, some of which he returned to Texas, contained a few discrepancies. A bureaucrat
steeped in formalism, Don Nemesio decreed that administrative
errors were not to be repeated![100]

Meanwhile, from Natchitoches, Apolinar Masmela informed
Captain Montero of Nacogdoches that he had contacted the Spanish consul to ascertain the latest status of the United States embargo on exports.[101] Subsequently, Félix Trudeaux, who operated
around the Red River country in Louisiana, notified Montero of
the lifting of the restriction on trade, but the Nacogdoches commander refrained from transmitting a large amount of money
across the Neutral Zone.[102] The purchasing agent, fearful of
bandits and filibusters, urged Montero to dispatch troops east of
the Sabine to disperse freebooters who preyed on supply cara-
vans.[103] The Nacogdoches captain, however, rather than provok-

[99] Peña to Salcedo, Revilla, July 20, 1812; Díaz de Bustamante to Salcedo,
Camargo, July 18, 1812, BA.
[100] Nemesio Salcedo to Governor of Texas [Salcedo], Chihuahua, July 11,
20, 1812, BA.
[101] Masmela to Montero, Natchitoches, July 9, 1812, BA.
[102] Montero to Salcedo, Nacogdoches, July 17, 1812, BA.
[103] Masmela to Montero, Natchitoches, July 22, 1812, BA.

ing the hostility of the Neutral Ground raiders, returned approximately six thousand pesos, an amount designated for Masmela, to Governor Salcedo in Béxar.[104]

Toward the end of July, Manuel Salcedo's problems intensified. If the threat of filibusters in Louisiana were not enough, a large band of Comanche warriors, reportedly about 130, attacked the San Marcos settlement and stole every horse in the vicinity. Governor Salcedo quickly asked Cristóbal Domínguez of the Presidio del Rio Grande for relief.[105] In less than a week the subinspector answered Salcedo's call for reinforcements by promising to send whatever presidiaries he could detach from his own unit.[106] With the newly appointed governor of Nuevo León, Díaz de Bustamante, Salcedo encountered modest difficulty in securing assistance. For one thing, the defender of Camargo contended that sporadic raids by rebellious Indians precluded his discharging the Texas contingent under his command.[107] Earlier, owing to a lack of hospital facilities on the lower Rio Grande, Díaz de Bustamante had sent Captain Luciano García to the infirmary in Béxar, after which he asked Salcedo to furnish a replacement! Not surprisingly, the Texas governor denied the request for a substitute officer and insisted on having the Béxar soldiers released from Camargo so that the city of San Antonio could be adequated defended. It was at this juncture that the liberator of Camargo, caught in a crossfire of words between Arredondo and the two Salcedos, disengaged fifty veteran fighters and allowed them to return to the Béxar garrison.[108]

In the interim, Manuel Salcedo, appealing to the Texas popu-

---

[104] The exact amount was 5,800 pesos (Montero to Salcedo, Nacogdoches, July 23, 1812, BA).

[105] Salcedo to Commander of Rio Grande, Béxar, July 20, 1812, BA.

[106] Domínguez to Salcedo, Presidio del Rio Grande, August 2, 1812, BA.

[107] Díaz de Bustamante to Salcedo, Camargo, August 1, 1812, BA.

[108] Díaz de Bustamante to Salcedo, Camargo, July 19, 1812; Salcedo to Díaz de Bustamante, Béxar, August 3, 6, 1812, BA.

lace to remain steadfastly loyal, denounced the revolt being carried on by Hidalgo's heirs as treasonous and entreated Hispanic
Texans to sacrifice their lives and property in defense of the king,
their religion, and the empire.[109] There was no question that
Salcedo recognized the magnitude of the danger that surrounded
his people, as his proclamation for continued support came on
the day following the execution of José Francisco Venegas, an
event that ominously impressed the spectators in Béxar.[110]

In Nacogdoches rapidly mounting tension drove Captain Montero into action. On July 30 he transferred command of the garrison to a subordinate and then led a detachment to the west bank
of the Sabine River to observe the filibusters' movements.[111]
Doubtlessly a sense of insecurity gripped the minds of Hispanic
defenders. Montero, impatient with imprecise information delivered by a soldier about allegedly having sighted two propagandists, confined the informant for failing to report clearly![112]
Hard pressed for a decision, the Nacogdoches commander on
August 6 held a council of war, during which Juan Manuel Zambrano, the subdeacon from San Antonio acting in a military capacity, advocated attacking the Neutral Ground. Although the
consensus was in favor of proceeding eastward,[113] the Hispanics,

109 Salcedo to the People and Garrisons of Texas, Béxar, July 31, 1812, BA.
110 After the execution, the commandant general wrote to Salcedo that the
entire proceedings should have been conducted in Nacogdoches, scene of the
apprehension, and not at the Texas capital. Salcedo replied that this could
have been arranged if an order to that effect had reached East Texas before
the prisoner's transfer to Béxar (José María Guadiana to Salcedo, Béxar,
August 1, 1812; Nemesio Salcedo to Governor of Texas [Salcedo], Chihuahua,
August 4, 1812; Salcedo to Commandant General [Nemesio Salcedo], Béxar,
August 5, 1812, BA).
111 Andrés de Santana to Salcedo, Nacogdoches, August 3, 1812; Montero
to Salcedo, Pasaje de los Aises, August 5, 1812, BA.
112 The unfortunate soldier was Ignacio Estrada (Montero to Salcedo,
Letter 202, Nacogdoches, August 5, 1812, BA).
113 Montero Diary, Arroyo de las Borregas, August 6, 1812, BA.

for lack of sufficient reserves, remained on their side of the river. Montero kept his men on constant watch as they waited for Governor Salcedo to send sizable reinforcements. The East Texas leader distrusted the apparent loyalty of Nacogdoches inhabitants so much in this crisis that he preferred to maintain his men in the field.[114] Montero's determination to hold the line was commendable, but it was inadequate to check the formidable invasion that moved toward him.

In early August, 1812, Spain's creaking defenses in East Texas collapsed when the vanguard of the Republican Army of the North crossed the Sabine River.[115] The filibusters' initial objective was Nacogdoches, a goal easily attainable because the majority of Montero's command was away from the fort. Virtually defenseless, the town fell on August 11 without resistance. Gutiérrez and Magee, followed by approximately 150 soldiers-of-fortune, had achieved the first part of their plan.[116]

The reaction of East Texas royalist officers was understandable. For the most part, misleading information confused their defensive posture. One officer, who had held out in Nacogdoches until the very end, notified Montero in the field that the filibusters' strength varied from three to seven hundred men.[117] Another informant, Sergeant Antonio Treviño, who had escaped from captivity in the Neutral Ground, declared that an enemy force numbering a thousand invaders was to land at Matagorda Bay.[118] Under these circumstances, Montero chose the better part of valor and retreated westward with his men to the Brazos River

[114] Montero to Salcedo, Pasaje de los Aises, August 8, 1812, BA.

[115] Henderson, "The Magee-Gutierrez Expedition," p. 46.

[116] Fisher, "American Influence upon Movement for Mexican Independence," pp. 470–471; Montero to Salcedo, Letter 208, Navasota, August 15, 1812, BA.

[117] Pedro Procela to Montero, Nacogdoches, August 11, 1812, BA.

[118] Pedro José de Aldape to Montero, Ojo de Agua de San Pedro, August 13, 1812, BA.

and beyond.[119] According to an account by Pedro José de Aldape, a loyalist sergeant who had stayed behind in Nacogdoches after Montero's withdrawal to organize the few remaining troops and to obtain horses, some East Texas settlers, finding themselves unprotected, went out to meet the oncoming rebels. Militarily, Hispanic organization deteriorated so fast during that second week in August that most of the enlisted men, riding to overtake Montero, deserted Sergeant Aldape's column and returned to Nacogdoches to join the filibusters.[120]

When Montero's courier sounded the alarm in Béxar, Governor Salcedo hastily sent a dispatch to Díaz de Bustamante in the lower Rio Grande.

I have this moment received word, under date of the 12th [of August], from the commander of Nacogdoches, who finds himself withdrawn to the Trinity River with part of his officers and troops. He reports that the Americans occupied Nacogdoches on the eleventh, the place having been abandoned because of the superiority of the American forces. Thus the dreaded day has arrived in which I see the ominous standard of revolt unfurled in that part of the kingdom.[121]

The Texas executive, as the overall provincial leader, stood firm as he decided on a course of action. From his companion-in-arms in Coahuila, Antonio Cordero, he asked for as many troops as could be spared and warned that the loss of Texas would mean the destruction of the rest of New Spain.[122] Next, he directed Captain Montero to continue his retreat into San Antonio, where a more manageable defense could be effected.[123] Regrettably, one

[119] Montero to Salcedo, Navasota, August 14, 1812, BA.

[120] Aldape Diary, Arroyo de Navasota, August 16, 1812, BA.

[121] Salcedo to Díaz de Bustamante, Béxar, August 17, 1812, BA; quoted in M'Caleb, "Gutierrez-Magee Expedition," pp. 223–224.

[122] Salcedo to Governor of Coahuila, Béxar, August 17, 1812, BA.

[123] Salcedo to Montero, Béxar, August 21, 1812, BA.

of Salcedo's staunchest supporters, Domínguez of the Río Grande presidio, in answer to superior orders temporarily repaired to Monclova,[124] but even with this setback the Texas governor resolved to face the challenge posed by the invaders. Cordero quickly replied that although his troop allotment was limited he would send reinforcements, and he went further in appealing to Don Nemesio to assist the beleaguered Salcedo.[125] Don Manuel, exercising every option available to him, wrote to a royalist sub-inspector of troops in San Luis Potosí, suggesting the possibilty of enlisting insurgents to repel the foreign invasion, but on second thought he dismissed the idea and counseled for a waiting period.[126] A Monterrey official in close contact with the sub-inspector reassured Salcedo that efforts were being made to call in Hispanic soldiers from various points south of the Río Grande for Texas duty.[127]

Meanwhile, in East Texas a Hispanic rear guard at Trinidad abandoned the outpost and fled westward. By mid-August the wide expanse from the Sabine to the Guadalupe River nominally belonged to the Republican Army of the North.[128] Furthermore, to undermine Spanish defenses in Béxar, Bernardo Gutiérrez launched a propaganda barrage. Finding a suitable distributor, however, was a problem. In early September the Mexican colonel sent Miguel Menchaca into Béxar with twelve copies of a fiery proclamation to deliver to an influential citizen, Luis Grande. In this instance, Gutiérrez' emissary failed; Governor Salcedo's alert defenders on September 22 arrested Grande and a Hispanic turncoat, Bergara, both of whom had seditious literature in their

---

[124] Domínguez to Salcedo, Presidio del Río Grande, August 5, 1812, BA.

[125] Cordero to Governor of Texas [Salcedo], Monclova, August 22, 1812, BA.

[126] Salcedo to José María Tovar, Béxar, August 23, 1812, BA.

[127] Bernardo Visel Guimbarda to Salcedo, Monterrey, August 25, 1812, BA.

[128] [Julia] Kathryn Garrett, "The First Constitution of Texas, April 17, 1813," *Southwestern Historical Quarterly*, 40, no. 4 (April, 1927), 298.

possession.[129] Indeed, Salcedo had just reason for dealing harshly
with those who succumbed to the guile of seditious documents.
The tenor of Gutiérrez' propaganda is evident in a proclamation
aimed at subverting the loyalty of capital residents:

> Soldiers and citizens of San Antonio de Béxar: It is more than a
> year since I left my country, during which time I have labored in-
> defatiguably for our good. I have overcome many difficulties, have
> made friends and have obtained means to aid us in throwing off the
> insulting yoke of the insolent despotism. Rise *en masse*, soldiers and
> citizens; unite in the holy cause of our country! . . .
> I am now marching to your succor with a respectable force of
> American volunteers who have left their homes and families to take
> up our cause, to fight for our liberty. They are the free descendents
> of the men who fought for the independence of the United States;
> . . . and as brothers and inhabitants of the same continent they have
> drawn their swords with a hearty good will in the defense of the
> cause of humanity; and in order to drive the tyrannous Europeans
> beyond the Atlantic.[130]

To attract volunteers for the filibustering expedition, Gutiérrez'
military leader, Colonel Magee, offered forty dollars a month
plus a Spanish league of land (4,428 acres). With such promises
and the enticing prospect of personal enrichment through plun-
dering, Magee gathered an assemblage, counting the vanguard
that captured Nacogdoches, of 780 recruits.[131] In mid-September,
Magee led the Republican Army to Trinidad, forded the river,
and for a month bivouacked in the vicinity.[132] During this interval there was constant movement between Nacogdoches and
Trinidad.

---

[129] M'Caleb, "Gutierrez-Magee Expedition," p. 227.

[130] Proclamation of Bernardo Gutiérrez, September 1, 1812, quoted in
Ibid., p. 226.

[131] Crimmins, "Magee," p. 95.

[132] Henderson, "Magee-Gutierrez Expedition," pp. 47–48.

The relative ease with which the transgressors from the Neutral Ground had penetrated into Spanish Texas probably convinced their principal leaders of their invincibility. Before they marched further into the interior, however, the sudden appearance of one of Zebulon M. Pike's 1807 associates, now emissary for the State Department of the United States, shattered the confidence of the Republican Army. The intruder was Dr. John Hamilton Robinson. On October 15, Magee's followers arrested the physician in Nacogdoches; the young colonel quickly summoned a council of war to decide what to do with the envoy whose presence cast a shadow on their plans.[133] During the discussion, the filibusters learned that Robinson's special mission required him to confer with the commandant general in Chihuahua about United States sincerity in wanting "to cooperate with Spain in proper policing of the frontier."[134] The next day, Magee's council released the envoy on the condition that he would sign a pledge to disclose to Salcedo's loyalists nothing of military significance about the filibustering expedition. When Robinson reached San Antonio de Béxar at the end of October, he encountered an unexpected but "cordial reception" from Colonels Salcedo and Herrera, to whom he casually mentioned the approximate position of the Republican Army near Trinidad.[135] To prevent the doctor from acquainting himself and others with the true nature of Hispanic defenses further west, Don Manuel detailed a six-man guard to escort the United States agent to the Presidio del Rio Grande; another security team assumed responsibility as far as Monclova.[136]

[133] Warren, *The Sword Was Their Passport*, pp. 37–40.
[134] Charles Carroll Griffin, *The United States and the Disruption of the Spanish Empire, 1810–1822: A Study of the Relations of the United States with Spain and with the Rebel Spanish Colonies*, p. 32.
[135] Warren, *The Sword Was Their Passport*, pp. 37–40.
[136] Salcedo to Commander of Presidio del Rio Grande [Domínguez], Béxar, October 27, 1812, BA.

After Robinson departed for Chihuahua, Salcedo regrouped his forces in San Antonio to meet the threat of an assault. Counting the soldiers the governor had recalled from La Bahía as well as whatever troops Antonio Cordero could spare, the Hispanic defenders of Texas numbered fifteen hundred men.[137] Don Manuel appointed Múñoz de Echavarría as lieutenant governor and commander of the military plaza in Béxar.[138] On November 2 he himself marched the majority of the Texas forces eastward to the left bank of the Guadalupe River crossing, where he carefully deployed them to ambush the invaders.[139]

The filibusters were not particularly anxious to engage the royalists until Gutiérrez' propaganda had scored an effect on Salcedo's partisans. But while Magee's raiders waited near the Trinity in late October, outriders captured a Hispanic wanderer who, probably under duress, revealed enough details about the Texas governor's countermeasures to prompt the expeditionary leaders to alter their plans. Accordingly, instead of continuing on the present course to attack the capital, the aggressors turned south by southwest to avoid Salcedo's trap on the Guadalupe River and proceeded to the coastal presidio of La Bahía. On November 7, the overwhelming numbers of the Republican Army easily compelled the token Spanish guard to flee for safety in San Antonio. Governor Salcedo anticipated a flanking movement; by a series of forced marches he pursued the trespassers to the Gulf settlement and began the siege of La Bahía.[140]

Salcedo's arrival at Espíritu Santo Bay put the invaders on the defensive. The governor from time to time directed frontal as-

---

[137] Hubert Howe Bancroft, *History of the North Mexican States and Texas*, II, 21–22.

[138] Salcedo to [Juan] José Múñoz de Echavarría, Béxar, November 1, 1812, BA.

[139] Henderson, "Magee-Gutierrez Expedition," pp. 47–48.

[140] *Ibid.*; Warren, *The Sword Was Their Passport*, p. 42.

saults on the fort, all of which proved ineffectual in dislodging the filibusters.[141] As the autumn days of November passed with no significant change in the position of the contesting forces, Don Manuel, equipped with fourteen pieces of artillery, divided his troops into four units, which he assigned to guard the opposite banks of the San Antonio River above and below La Bahía. To counter the royalist move, the filibusters haphazardly piled earthen mounds on all sides of the presidio to protect their limited artillery.[142]

The siege worked to the advantage of the royalists. Cordero of Coahuila sent Vicente Flores with 40 experienced fighters to strengthen Salcedo's encampment at La Bahía.[143] Later, Don Antonio dispatched ten boxes of gunpowder and, more importantly, ordered Cristóbal Domínguez to lead 150 men to bolster Don Manuel's defenses. Indeed, the Rio Grande presidial commander wasted little time in going to the Texas governor's assistance.[144]

In the bleak days of the siege, blood ties surmounted bureaucratic indifference; Don Nemesio sent a personal note to Salcedo wishing him success in the campaign against the invaders and expressing confidence in the governor's ability to conduct a creditable stand. Still later, the commandant general, sympathiz-

[141] Bancroft, *History of the North Mexican States and Texas*, II, 21–22.

[142] H[enderson R.] Yoakum, *History of Texas: From Its First Settlement in 1685 to Its Annexation to the United States in 1846*, I, 162–163. Hereinafter cited as Yoakum, *Texas*.

[143] Cordero to Governor of Texas [Salcedo], Monclova, November 1, 1812, BA.

[144] Cordero to Governor of Texas [Salcedo], Monclova, November 20, 23, 1812; Domínguez to Salcedo, Presidio del Rio Grande, November 25, 1812, BA. In Béxar, the lieutenant governor took precautionary measures in the defense of the capital by assigning a corporal and six men to operate each of the artillery pieces placed at the street intersections. Among the noncombatants, Padre José Darío Zambrano was an active defender (Múñoz de Echavarría to Salcedo, Béxar, November 17, 1812, BA).

ing with Don Manuel for Hispanic reverses at La Bahía, urged Salcedo onward by stating that in the end the Texas governor would win the battle.[145]

The reversals to which Don Nemesio referred pertained to three unsuccessful assaults on the fort in November, after which Salcedo ceased hostilities and invited Republican Army leaders to confer with him about a truce. Henderson R. Yoakum, nineteenth-century Texas historian, described the meeting:

> Previous to the last assault, for some unknown cause, a cessation of hostilities for three days had been agreed upon. During this time the officers of the two armies extended to each other civilties due among gentlemen. Colonel Magee, by invitation, dined with Salcedo in the quarters of the latter. Between them an agreement was made, . . . to the effect that the fort should be delivered up, the Americans to return home without their arms, but to be supplied on the march by provisions by Salcedo.[146]

In exchange for allowing Anglo-American filibusters to retire from Texas, Salcedo demanded that Mexican insurgents in the Republican Army be surrendered to Spanish authorities. Magee, when he unfolded the conditions of the truce within the fort, faced serious opposition to his leadership from the ranks. The soldiers-of-fortune unceremoniously rejected the young colonel's plan. Consequently, the cease-fire ended fruitlessly as the opposing sides resumed hostilities on November 23, 1812.[147]

In the wintry days of December, the sporadic fighting slowed down but the stalemate continued. The Hispanics, of course, had access to limited reinforcements, whereas the filibusters began to realize that their position, however secure, was untenable.

---

[145] Nemesio Salcedo to Salcedo, Chihuahua, November 10, December 8, 1812, BA.

[146] Yoakum, *Texas*, I, 164.

[147] Warren, *The Sword Was Their Passport*, p. 43.

Worse yet, Colonel Magee, on whom military operations depended, contracted an illness that gradually drained his energy until he died on February 6, 1813.[148] Magee's death momentarily staggered the Republican Army. Bernardo Gutiérrez, whose self-importance rose appreciably, later bitterly denounced the dead colonel's leadership.

During this time [at La Bahía] we suffered every kind of calamity, the greatest of all being this: the American colonel Magee, who was my second in command, was a man of military genius but very cowardly; and moreover, he was a vile traitor . . . in promising to sell me to Salcedo for fifteen thousand pesos and the position of colonel in the Royalist ranks. For this reason he was always opposed to my using strategy and other means by which I could have harmed the enemy greatly. But the divine Omnipotence who always favored us, permitted this villain to fall sick and die, as a result of some poison which he had taken to avoid being shot.[149]

Magee's untimely death was propitious for Salcedo. But four months of arduous attempts to storm the fort had exhausted the royalists. After the death of Magee, Don Manuel directed two determined attacks, both of which cost him about three hundred casualties. The victory that the loyalists desperately needed seemed to elude them. Realizing the futility of continuing the

[148] Carlos E. Castañeda, *Our Catholic Heritage in Texas, 1519–1936*, VI, 95. Among Texas historians much controversy surrounds the death of Augustus William Magee, with respect to both cause and date. Castañeda rejected the apparent suicide theory, but others, such as Garrett and Warren, accepted the account of United States special agent William Shaler. Still another historian, Colonel Martin Lalor Crimmins, who tended to laud the former West Point officer, cited a later date but omitted altogether a discussion of the nature of the demise (Garrett, *Green Flag over Texas*, p. 173; Warren, *The Sword Was Their Passport*, p. 45; Crimmins, "Magee," p. 98).

[149] J. B. Gutiérrez de Lara to the Mexican Congress; Account of Progress of Revolution from Beginning, August 1, 1815, in Charles Adams Gulick, Jr., and Katherine Elliott (eds.), *The Papers of Mirabeau Buonaparte Lamar*, I, 12.

struggle, especially when their manpower and supplies had dwindled to a dangerously low point, Salcedo and Herrera, now totally unsupported by the neighboring provinces, lifted the siege on February 19, 1813. Their disorderly withdrawal to San Antonio de Béxar resulted in mass defections to the side of the invaders.[150]

Salcedo's rule stood on the edge of disaster, but doggedly the two Spanish colonels managed to rally enough royalist sympathizers —both civilian and military—from Béxar to allow them to make a final stand near the capital. Two days after the royalists pulled away from La Bahía, the Republican Army, augmented by new volunteers from the Neutral Ground and by Indian warriors, evacuated the stone fortress and marched north along the San Antonio River. Samuel Kemper of Virginia assumed command of Gutiérrez' motley army. On March 28, as the filibusters approached Salado Creek, approximately three leagues southeast of the city of Béxar, Colonel Herrera, leading fifteen hundred regular troops and one thousand militiamen, sallied forth to engage the enemy.[151]

The Battle of Salado—identified also as the Battle of Rosillo— resulted in a devastating defeat for Herrera's followers. The Anglo-Americans, cleverly using Indian auxiliaries to charge directly into the Spanish cavalry, quickly outflanked the royalists.[152] Yoakum vividly described the military engagement:

About nine miles from San Antonio there was a ridge, of gentle slope, dividing the waters of the San Antonio River and the Salado. The side of this river next to the San Antonio, from the crest of the road, consisted of prairie; the side bordering the Salado was covered

---

[150] Castañeda, *Our Catholic Heritage in Texas*, VI, 96; Warren, *The Sword Was Their Passport*, p. 45.

[151] Henderson, "The Magee-Gutierrez Expedition," pp. 50–51.

[152] Sidney Lanier, "San Antonio de Bexar," in *San Antonio de Bexar: A Guide and History*, comp. and ed. William Corner, p. 78.

with *chapparal*, a species of thick underwood. In this chapparal the Spaniards were lying in ambush. They were discovered by riflemen, who were marching on the crest of the ridge, and who opened fire upon them. They [the Spaniards] immediately formed, and presented themselves to the American army about four hundred yards below. The Spanish line, in the center of which were twelve pieces of artillery, crowned the crest of the ridge for three quarters of a mile.[153]

Herrera's troops fought gallantly for fifteen or twenty minutes, then suddenly broke their line of defense and fled aimlessly for Béxar. The filibusters, unable to control the Indian auxiliaries, permitted them to commit wanton atrocities upon the fugitives. Clearly, Salado Creek was the invaders' first decisive victory. The royalists suffered heavy losses: 330 men killed and 60 others taken captive. The republicans reported 6 killed and 26 wounded.[154] Flushed with success, the assailants pursued the fleeing royalists toward Béxar.

Salcedo's withdrawal from La Bahía and Herrera's defeat at Salado Creek caused immeasurable consternation in the Texas capital. Earlier, Dr. Robinson, returning to the United States from an unproductive conference in Chihuahua, had reported that utter chaos pervaded San Antonio.[155] Manuel Salcedo, in Spain's darkest hour in Texas, felt genuine compassion for the people who faithfully supported the king's interests. In their behalf, he drafted a twelve-point plan for an honorable surrender. The first four conditions asked for humane treatment of noncombatants with respect to their lives, property, and religious convictions. The remainder of the provisions pertained to the royalist army; the most salient of these asked that the soldiers be allowed to

[153] Yoakum, *Texas*, I, 166–167.
[154] Henderson, "The Magee-Gutierrez Expedition," p. 51.
[155] Warren, *The Sword Was Their Passport*, pp. 41–42; Haggard, "The Neutral Ground between Louisiana and Texas," p. 1054.

retire from the city in full possession of their arms and equipment. On April 1 the governor dispatched three messengers to
convey the plan of capitulation to Gutiérrez, who was bivouacked
at Mission Concepción. Two of the envoys the Mexican colonel
siezed as hostages; the third returned to Béxar with Gutiérrez'
curt refusal of the conditions. Moreover, the rebel from Revilla
warned Salcedo not to cause further delay lest there be a complete breakdown of the standard rules of warfare. Shortly thereafter, the filibusters moved closer to the city along the east bank
of the river to the secularized Mission San Antonio de Valero.
That night Governor Salcedo and Colonel Herrera, fatalists to
the very end, invited the Anglo-American officers to dine with
them in Béxar.[156] It is entirely possible that the Spanish stalwarts,
considering the circumstances in which they found themselves,
intended to create dissension in the Republican Army. To an
extent they succeeded in reducing the antipathy of some filibusters toward Hispanicism, but not sufficiently to change the outcome. In any case, the two Texas leaders maintained a gentlemanly decorum that undoubtedly impressed their guests.

The next morning Governor Salcedo, followed by fourteen
members of his staff, strode out of the Casas Reales into the
spacious military plaza for the formal surrender of the province.
The scene was high drama. With matchless dignity Don Manuel
tried to present his sword to two Anglo-American officers; both
men, for reasons of protocol, refrained from accepting it and
gestured toward Gutiérrez. The suggestion momentarily un-
hinged Salcedo. Taking his sword by the handle, he pointedly
stuck it in the ground and stepped back to join his colleagues.
Gutiérrez, who obviously lacked style, picked up the swaying
weapon.[157] Symbolic of the transfer of power, the green banner

156 Castañeda, *Our Catholic Heritage in Texas*, VI, 97–98.
157 Yoakum, *Texas*, I, 168.

of the Republican Army of the North replaced the brilliant standard of the Spanish monarch. For Salcedo and Herrera, the humiliation was a repeat performance of an earlier experience. Following the surrender, Gutiérrez' partisans released all political prisoners, most of whom swelled the ranks of the expeditionary force. After establishing a provisional government, with himself as generalissimo and governor, Gutiérrez appointed a junta to deliberate pending charges against the royalist officials, principally the two colonels. To ensure an appropriate verdict the Mexican revolutionist then stacked the committee with members of a local family—the Menchacas—who were avowed sympathizers of Mexican independence and vehement opponents of royalism. Not surprisingly, the junta adjudged the accused guilty of treachery to the Hidalgo movement and condemned them to death. But because of protests raised by Anglo-American officers, Gutiérrez' confidants seemingly yielded and agreed to confine the royalists away from Béxar, possibly as far as New Orleans.[158]

Under this illusion, on the night of April 3, the prisoners, with their hands tied behind their backs, readily submitted to the orders of Antonio Delgado, a rebel captain in charge of sixty Mexican soldiers. All mounted, the group rode out of town in a southeasterly direction toward Salado Creek. Upon arriving at the site where the Battle of Rosillo had occurred, the guards forcibly dismounted the royalists, then insulted them with disparaging words, and, finally, as if by design, drew knives from their belts and swiftly assassinated Salcedo, Herrera, and the other aides. Leaving the mutilated bodies strewn in the field, Captain Delgado and his fellow assassins returned to Béxar the

---

[158] *Ibid.*; Bancroft, *History of the North Mexican States and Texas*, II, 23–24; *Lamar Papers*, II, 23–24 and IV, pt. 2, 7; Warren, *The Sword Was Their Passport*, p. 50.

next morning and in a haughty manner announced the brutal deed to the republicans in the crowded military plaza.[159]

Ironically, Salcedo's assassination shocked the bureaucracy of New Spain into planning an aggressive reconquest of Texas, for the reasons that the dead governor had advocated during his stewardship. Months later, on August 28, 1813, one of the Zambrano brothers—Padre José Darío—interred Salcedo's last remains in "the first crypt" of San Fernando Church "with watch and mass and nine stations and the catafalque."[160]

During his governorship of nearly five years, Manuel María de Salcedo had personified nineteenth-century royalism on the northeastern edge of the Spanish borderlands. To be sure, Don Manuel's private differences with his uncle affected what otherwise might have been an efficient performance of duty, but Salcedo had struggled consistently to reform the inner structure of his administration so as to withstand the assaults of Spain's enemies in North America.

Unlike those who preceded him in Texas, Salcedo looked on his assignment as an opportunity to plan and execute a meaningful program, but he unfortunately failed to win the essential endorsement of the commandant general. Don Manuel was a

---

[159] The other Hispanic victims were Gerónimo Herrera, Múñoz de Echavarría, José Matéos, José Groscochea, Francisco Pereira, Juan Ignacio Arrambide, Gregorio Amador, and Antonio López. Four Mexicans who supported the royalist rule also lost their lives (Yoakum, *Texas*, I, 169–170; *Lamar Papers*, IV, pt. 2, 7–8; Warren, *The Sword Was Their Passport*, p. 50; Henderson, "The Magee-Gutierrez Expedition," p. 52).

[160] By this time, Salcedo's wife, María Guadalupe, had died, probably in New Orleans, where she had sought refuge from the violence of the revolution. No document has been uncovered to determine the fate of Salcedo's daughter, Mariquita, who accompanied her mother to Louisiana. Simón de Herrera left a mourning widow, María Josefa (Chabot, *Texas in 1811*, p. 146; Entierros, San Fernando Parish, 1802–1817, Foja 102, Numero 539, Dn. Manuel de Salcedo Governador de esta capital. San Fernando Archives, San Antonio, Texas).

Hispanic with ideas who valiantly tried to safeguard the province and the prerogatives of the gubernatorial office. Undeniably, he believed in the soundness of his proposals, but, to a degree, he was artless in confronting the bureaucracy that exercised jurisdiction over them. Still, the governor was unflinchingly loyal to the Spanish empire in opposing first the Hidalgo insurgents and then the filibusters. The contest, when reduced to simpler terms, was Salcedo versus the violent forces of change. Against the thrust of revolutionists from the Rio Grande Valley and the aggression of Anglo-American frontiersmen from the Mississippi Valley, he stood virtually defenseless. Truly, Salcedo of Texas was a tragic cavalier.

7. HISPANIC TEXAS AFTER SALCEDO

THE ASSASSINATION of Governor Salcedo set off rever-
berations on both sides of the Rio Grande. Almost immediately Captain Delgado's criminal deed, which
Gutiérrez' partisans justified as an act of personal re-
venge, alienated most of the Anglo-American leaders in Béxar,
who avowed that murder did not represent their interests in the
Republican Army. South of the Rio Grande, Hispanic officials
promptly organized an expedition to reconquer Texas and to
evict the intruders who had dared to proclaim the province a
republic.

In an effort to avenge Salcedo and Herrera, the bureaucracy
shifted the center of authority from Chihuahua to Monterrey.
Significantly, the crisis in Texas compelled Viceroy Félix Calleja
in 1813 to create a new administrative unit—the commandancy
general of the Eastern Interior Provinces—and promoted Joaquín de Arredondo to administer the office.[1]

---

[1] For a discussion of the intricacies of Arredondo's professional advancement, see Julia Kathryn Garrett, *Green Flag over Texas: A Story of the Last
Years of Spain in Texas*, pp. 206–210. In July, 1813, Salcedo's uncle, Don

One of Arredondo's subordinates was the redeemed royalist, Lieutenant Colonel Ignacio Elizondo of the Laredo presidio, who doubtlessly was among the first to learn of Salcedo's assassination from Béxar fugitives. In early June, ordered to advance as far as the Frio River to keep the filibusters under surveillance, Elizondo led approximately three thousand ill-trained troops to the designated location, but, in defiance of authority, he crossed the river. As he approached the Texas capital, the colonel, who seemingly had a propensity for theatrical militarism, camped on the west bank of Alazán Creek on June 16 and there challenged the Republican Army. Evidently Elizondo, recalling his success at the Wells of Baján two years earlier, expected the mere presence of his large group to disperse the filibusters. To be sure, Don Ignacio's sudden arrival surprised the invaders at a time when they lacked a leader. The disorder in Béxar quickly subsided, however, when Henry Perry took command of Gutiérrez' army. After nightfall the republicans stealthily moved out of the city toward Elizondo's encampment. At dawn, with the sunrays behind them, the Anglo-Americans stormed across the Alazán "with firmness and regularity."[2] An anonymous account related the battle:

From the towers of the Catholic Church [San Fernando], a party of curious boys, . . . were regarding through glasses the glittering army and burnished sheen, and listening appalled to the booming

Nemesio, relinquished the commandancy general, reorganized as the Western Interior Provinces, to Bernardo Bonavía. The one-time deputy commandant general opted to administer the new office from his provincial headquarters in Durango and had overall responsibility for Nueva Vizcaya, Sonora, and Nuevo México. The Eastern Interior Provinces, governed by Arredondo, consisted of Coahuila, Texas, Nuevo León, and Nuevo Santander (Luis Navarro García, *Las Provincias Internas en el siglo XIX*, pp. 74–76).

[2] Harry McCorry Henderson, "The Magee-Gutierrez Expedition," *Southwestern Historical Quarterly*, 55, no. 1 (July, 1951), 53–54.

sound of the cannon. After a combat of four hours, Elisando [*sic*] was defeated. He retreated hurriedly having sustained a loss of four hundred in killed and wounded. He likewise left some prisoners.[3]

Retreating toward the Rio Grande, Elizondo arrived at Laredo, where he met the main force under Arredondo. The blistering reprimand the commandant general administered so humiliated the colonel that never again did he disobey a direct order. Arredondo then reported to the viceregal office on his progress:

When he [Elizondo] had joined me, I united his infantry and cavalry with mine to form a single army. . . . This made the total . . . eighteen hundred and thirty men, consisting of a force of six hundred and ninety-five infantry and eleven hundred and ninety-five cavalry. We continued our march . . . after having halted for a few days' rest so that. . . . we might explain and teach the most necessary and indispensable formations and maneuvers in an action or battle. It was necessary to do so, as Elizondo's men lacked this training.[4]

Even with the unavoidable delays, Arredondo's army clearly presented a formidable threat to the filibusters in Texas. Seemingly unconcerned, Gutiérrez, in the aftermath of the rebel victory at Alazán, remained in control of affairs until the arrival in July of his chief propagandist, José Álvarez de Toledo, who lost no time in undermining the Mexican colonel's position with the soldiers. Álvarez de Toledo's flamboyant style quickly won Anglo-American supporters to his bid for leadership. On August 4, 1813, at a time when unity was essential for survival, the

[3] Charles Adams Gulick, Jr., and Katherine Elliott (eds.), *The Papers of Mirabeau Buonaparte Lamar*, IV, pt. 2, 9.

[4] Mattie Austin Hatcher (trans.), "Joaquin de Arredondo's Report of the Battle of the Medina, August 18, 1813," *Quarterly of the Texas State Historical Association*, 11, no. 3 (January, 1908), 220–221. Hereinafter cited as "Arredondo's Report."

Álvarez faction succeeded in ousting Gutiérrez from power. Crestfallen, the revolutionist from Revilla retired to the United States. At the Texas capital, the new leader, after renaming the motley group the Republican Army of North Mexico, committed a tactical error that lowered morale and created suspicion and dissension. With almost total disregard for friendship and mutual trust among the filibusters, Álvarez divided the military along ethnic lines: the Mexicans and Indians constituted one fighting unit and the Anglo-Americans the other.[5]

Reorganization of the filibustering expedition came at a most inauspicious time. It was common knowledge in Béxar that Arredondo's sizable army had traversed the Nueces River and had bivouacked temporarily on the Laredo–San Antonio road. Álvarez de Toledo found himself in a quandary. To lead the republicans into combat, he needed the cooperation of the officers. Moreover, the low morale caused by the regrouping further complicated the situation. After several futile attempts to take the army into the field, the pamphleteer from Cuba partially overcame resistance to his leadership—among other ways, by sponsoring a dance for his subordinates. Finally, on August 15,

[5] Henderson, "The Magee-Gutierrez Expedition," pp. 54–55. On the eve of the battle of Alazán Creek, Doña María José Uribe de Gutiérrez joined her husband in San Antonio. After Álvarez de Toledo's usurpation of power, the deposed Guitérrez gathered his family and left the Texas capital on August 6, 1813, bound for exile in Louisiana, where for several years he became involved in planning a number of filibustering expeditions, none of which materialized. In 1824, with the culmination of Mexican independence, Gutiérrez returned to his hometown of Revilla after an absence of nearly thirteen years and assumed the governorship of Tamaulipas. In December, 1825, the national government, in recognition of services rendered, appointed Don Bernardo commandant general of the Eastern Interior Provinces, an assignment that he discharged until a replacement succeeded him a year later. On May 13, 1841, Bernardo Gutiérrez de Lara died in the home of his daughter in the town of Santiago (Rie Jarratt, *Gutiérrez de Lara, Mexican-Texan: The Story of a Creole Hero*; pp. 46–67).

the Republican Army marched out of the southeast portal of San Antonio and within two days reached the Medina River.[6]

Moving up from the south, General Arredondo, informed by scouts of the presence of a large body of men near the Medina, halted his army and dispatched Ignacio Elizondo with 180 cavalrymen to reconnoiter the terrain ahead. This time Elizondo obeyed Arredondo's instructions not to engage the enemy forces "unless he thought himself strong enough to inflict an exemplary punishment upon them; and, if not, to keep up a slow fire while retreating to give me prompt information that I might make my plans." With almost precise timing, Elizondo's ploy worked to the advantage of the Hispanics. Mistaking the reconnaissance party for the entire Spanish command, Álvarez de Toledo's republicans eagerly pursued the retreating cavalrymen across the Medina. Arredondo (with the subjectivity permitted a victorious field commander) gave the following report of the battle:

Believing that they were already glorious victors and masters of the field, and had only to take the spoils . . . the republicans advanced bravely yet blindly; but found themselves confronted by the main body of our army formed in line for attack, with the artillery placed on the flanks of the cavalry. This surprised the rabble, and halted them for the purpose of retreating. They did this, being aided by the great number of oaks with which the country was covered. . . . So there was a very hard fought battle, reaching the extreme of having their artillery placed [within] forty paces of ours. . . . After three and a half hours of this determined and hard fought conflict, it was seen that victory was on our side; for the most obstinate Anglo-Americans had been completely routed. Seeing this, I ordered the music to start up and my drummer to beat the reveille. This had such an effect on my troops and reanimated them so much that it

[6] Harris Gaylord Warren, "José Álvarez de Toledo's Initiation as a Filibuster, 1811–1813," *Hispanic American Historical Review*, 20, no. 1 (February, 1940), 77–78.

seemed as if they were going to advance. Confusion now seized upon the enemy; and they began to abandon their artillery. . . . Consequently, after four hours of this bloody battle we were masters of the enemy's ground.[7]

What began as a slow withdrawal by the filibusters soon turned into runaway chaos. Colonel Elizondo, trying to erase the memory of his defeat at Alazán, energetically chased the fleeing rebels "with sword and lance" into Béxar. By the time the Spanish cavalrymen entered the environs of the capital, probably late in the afternoon of August 18, the invaders already had evacuated the city, leaving only panic-stricken noncombatants. Elizondo efficiently pacified the town in preparation for the commandant general's triumphant entry two days later.

Arredondo's retribution was without mercy. His soldiers indiscriminately arrested about seven hundred male residents and lodged them in whatever facilities could be used as detention wards. In the quarters occupied by the parish priests, the army confined more than three hundred individuals, eighteen of whom suffocated "in the scorching heat of summer." Women suspected of being in sympathy with the rebellion—mothers, wives, and daughters of insurgents—suffered great indignities. In a makeshift jail near the south end of the main plaza, called La Quinta, the female prisoners labored long hours daily converting "twenty-four bushels of corn into *tortillas*" to feed Arredondo's occupation forces.[8]

---

[7] "Arredondo's Report," pp. 222–225.

[8] *Lamar Papers*, IV, pt. 2, 10–11. According to a reliable account of the military aspects of the filibustering expedition, the Hispanics, after the Battle of Medina, captured 112 republicans, all of whom faced the firing squad. Elizondo subsequently apprehended another 215 fugitives in and around Béxar, most of whom went to jail. At La Bahía the Spaniards, under Captain Luciano García, seized over 300 prisoners. Not counting Elizondo's later executions at the Trinity River, the list of rebel casualties numbered 1,000. Reportedly, the Hispanics estimated their losses as minimal: 55 killed in

Without doubt, the commandant general's vengeance on
Spanish Texas was swift and hard. Confiscation, detention, and
execution were the methods he used to restore royalist authority.
Illustrative of the impact that the reconquest had on the citizenry
of Béxar is a petition of Doña Luisa de Luna to the *cabildo*, part
of which, written by a scribe, read:

> because my husband Vicente Travieso was one of those carried away
> by caprices and want of judgment to help the iniquitous party of the
> insurrection . . . they [the royalists] have sequestrated everything
> that belonged to my husband and me . . . I have been reduced to
> misery and want, I and four small children . . . So I apply to the
> benignity and powerful protection of your highness to order that,
> moved by pity you will have the charity to give to me one of the
> rooms of the house known as mine, one of the small cows so that my
> unhappy and unfortunate children will have something to nourish
> them.

On this occasion the government made restitution, but generally
this was the exception and not the rule.[9]

After the Spanish army crushed the filibusters at Medina, the
survivors—including Álvarez de Toledo, Henry Perry, and other
officers—desperately raced along the Camino Real for the eastern
border to escape the wrath of Arredondo. Fear and confusion
seized the minds of the runaways as Ignacio Elizondo's cavalry
surrounded a group of families at the Trinity River, where, on
the spot, the colonel dispensed instant justice to more than one
hundred male refugees.[10]

As the Trinity River prisoners occupied the attention of the
Hispanics, farther east Álvarez de Toledo realized the futility of

---

combat, 178 wounded, and 2 missing in action (Henderson, "The Magee-
Gutierrez Expedition," p. 60).

[9] Maury Maverick (cooperating sponsor), *Old Villita*, p. 10.

[10] *Lamar Papers*, IV, pt. 2, 11.

making a final stand in Nacogdoches and took a group of about three hundred fugitives, including women and children, across the Sabine River into the Neutral Ground. Eventually most of the filibusters who successfully outran their pursuers drifted into Natchitoches, where a few adventurous souls, despite the disaster of Medina, still boasted of a renewed invasion of Texas.[11] General Arredondo, aware of the Neutral Ground's potential danger to Spanish interests, warned would-be filibusters that in his judgment the Sabine River was under Hispanic jurisdiction and that all interlopers who dared to cross it would be shot if captured.[12]

For a period of about three years the commandant general's declaration curbed unauthorized penetrations into Texas, but the unprotected coastline—especially Galveston Island—invited transgressions. By 1816 the island teemed with filibusters and pirates. Francisco Xavier Mina and Luis Aury, joined by Henry Perry of the ill-fated Gutiérrez-Magee expedition, raided Spanish maritime commerce in the Gulf of Mexico for a few months. Then Mina and Perry invaded the coastal area south of the Rio Grande. In 1817 they split their forces, and Perry marched north to La Bahía in Texas. Unsuccessful in their attempt to capture the presidio, the filibusters, pursued by a sizable Hispanic contingent, tried to reach Nacogdoches. Thwarted again by the Spaniards, the invaders fought a losing battle in which the leader, grievously wounded, committed suicide. Four ragged survivors, who eluded capture, recounted in Louisiana the destruction of another filibustering expedition.

The successor to the piratical haven on Galveston Island was

[11] J. Villasana Haggard, "The Neutral Ground between Louisiana and Texas, 1806–1821," *Louisiana Historical Quarterly*, 28, no. 4 (October, 1945), 1055.

[12] Lillian E. Fisher, "American Influence upon the Movement for Mexican Independence," *Mississippi Valley Historical Review*, 18, no. 3 (December, 1923), 471.

Jean Lafitte, who confined his hostilities mainly to the Gulf waters. A more filibustering type was Dr. James Long, who, in June, 1819, established a short-lived republic in Nacogdoches. The following year the physician launched a second abortive expedition into Texas, but by then the Spanish structure had nearly collapsed.[13]

Antonio María Martínez was the last full-fledged governor of Hispanic Texas. Between 1813, the end of Salcedo's rule, and 1817, the beginning of Martínez' administration, five different royalists occupied the gubernatorial office in an ad interim capacity—Cristóbal Domínguez, Benito de Armiñan, Mariano Varela, Ignacio Pérez, and Manuel Pardo.[14] However, it fell to Governor Martínez to witness the closing of the Spanish period in Texas. In spite of his efforts to improve the condition of the province, Don Antonio, like Salcedo before him, was unable to persuade the bureaucracy to think in positive terms. No doubt Commandant General Arredondo's harsh reconquest so debilitated the province that the transition from Spanish to Mexican authority was virtually painless to the inhabitants.

[13] Odie B. Faulk, *The Last Years of Spanish Texas, 1778–1821*, pp. 136–139.
[14] H. Bailey Carroll (ed.), "Texas Collection: Governors of Texas, 1778–1822," *Southwestern Historical Quarterly*, 46, no. 4 (April, 1963), 593–594. For a summary of Martínez' career, see Virginia H. Taylor, *The Letters of Antonio Martinez: Last Spanish Governor of Texas, 1817–1822.*

BIBLIOGRAPHY

ARCHIVES

Austin. The University of Texas Archives. Eugene C. Barker Texas History Center. Béxar Archives.
Austin. The Texas State Library Archives. Nacogdoches Archives.
Washington, D.C. National Archives. Record Group 107. 1808–1814.
San Antonio. Bexar County Archives. San Fernando Archives.

PUBLISHED LETTERS, DOCUMENTS, AND PAPERS

Benson, Nettie Lee (ed. and trans.). *Report that Dr. Miguel Ramos de Arizpe Priest of Borbon, and Deputy in the Present General and Special Cortes of Spain for the Province of Coahuila One of the Four Eastern Interior Provinces of the Kingdom of Mexico Presents to the August Congress on the Natural, Political, and Civil Condition of the Provinces of Coahuila, Nuevo León, Nuevo Santander, and Texas of the Four Eastern Interior Provinces of the Kingdom of Mexico.* The University of Texas Institute of Latin-American Studies, vol. 9. Austin: University of Texas Press, 1950.
Carroll, H. Bailey, and J. Villasana Haggard (eds. and trans.). *Three New Mexico Chronicles: The Exposición of Don Pedro Bautista Pino 1812; the Ojeada of Lic. Antonio Barriero 1832; and the additions by Don José Agustín de Escudero, 1849.* Albuquerque: The Quivira Society, 1942.
Coues, Elliott (ed.). *The Expeditions of Zebulon Montgomery Pike,*

to *Headwaters of the Mississippi River, through Louisiana Territory, and in New Spain, during the Years 1805–6–7.* 3 vols. New
York: Francis P. Harper, 1895.

Faulk, Odie (ed. and trans.). "A Description of Texas in 1803."
Southwestern Historical Quarterly 66, no. 4 (April, 1963): 513–
515.

Frétellière, Auguste. "Adventures of a Castrovillian," in *Castro-Ville
and Henry Castro—Empresario.* Julia Nott Waugh. San Antonio:
Standard Printing Company, 1934.

Garrett, Julia Kathryn (ed.). "Letters and Documents: Dr. John
Sibley and the Louisiana-Texas Frontier, 1803–1814." *Southwestern Historical Quarterly* 48, no. 1 (July, 1944): 67–70.

Guice, C. Norman (ed. and trans.). "Texas in 1804." *Southwestern
Historical Quarterly* 59, no. 1 (July, 1955): 46–56.

Gulick, Charles Adams, Jr., and Katherine Elliott (eds.). *The Papers
of Mirabeau Buonaparte Lamar.* 6 vols. Austin: Texas State Library, 1921–1928.

Hatcher, Mattie Austin (trans.). "Joaquin de Arredondo's Report of
the Battle of the Medina, August 18, 1813." *Quarterly of the Texas
State Historical Association* 11, no. 3 (January, 1908): 220–236.

[Rodríguez, J. María.] *Rodriguez Memoirs of Early Texas.* San Antonio: Passing Show Printing Company, 1913.

Taylor, Virginia H. *The Letters of Antonio Martínez: Last Spanish
Governor of Texas, 1817–1822.* Austin: Texas State Library, 1957.

*Transcriptions of Manuscript Collections of Louisiana. No. 1. The
Favrot Papers, 1799–1801.* The Louisiana Historical Records Survey, Division of Community Service Programs, Works Projects
Administration, vol. 6. New Orleans: Tulane University of Louisiana, 1941.

THESES AND DISSERTATIONS

Kimbrough, Birch Duke. "The Spanish Regime in Texas." Master's
thesis, East Texas State Teachers College, 1939.

King, Nyal C. "Captain Antonio Gil Y'Barbo: Founder of Modern
Nacogdoches, 1729–1809." Master's thesis, Stephen F. Austin State
Teachers College, 1949.

Miller, Margaret. "Survey of Civil Government of San Antonio, Texas, 1731–1948." Master's thesis, St. Mary's University, 1948.

Smith, Dick. "The Development of Local Government Units in Texas." Ph.D. dissertation, Harvard University, 1938.

BOOKS

Alessio Robles, Vito. *Coahuila y Texas en la época colonial.* Mexico City: Editorial Cultura, 1938.

Bancroft, Hubert Howe. *History of the North Mexican States and Texas.* 2 vols. San Francisco: The History Company, 1889.

Binkley, William Campbell. *The Expansionist Movement in Texas, 1826–1850.* University of California Publications in History, vol. 13. Berkeley: University of California Press, 1925.

Blackmar, Frank W. *Spanish Institutions of the Southwest.* Baltimore: The Johns Hopkins Press, 1891.

Bolton, Herbert Eugene. *Texas in the Middle Eighteenth Century: Studies in Spanish Colonial History and Administration.* New York: Russell & Russell, Inc., 1962.

Brinckerhoff, Sidney B., and Odie B. Faulk. *Lancers for the King: A Study of the Frontier Military System of Northern New Spain.* Phoenix: Arizona Historical Foundation, 1965.

Castañeda, Carlos E. *Our Catholic Heritage in Texas: 1519–1936.* 7 vols. Austin: Von Boeckmann-Jones Company, 1936–1958.

Castillo Ledón, Luis. *Hidalgo: La vida del héroe.* 2 vols. Mexico City: Talleres Gráficos de la Nación, 1949.

Chabot, Frederick C. (ed.). *Texas in 1811: The Las Casas and Sambrano Revolutions.* San Antonio: The Yanaguana Society, 1941.

Coan, Charles F. *A History of New Mexico.* 3 vols. Chicago and New York: The American Historical Society, Inc., 1925.

Covián Martínez, Vidal. *Don José Bernardo Maximiliano Gutiérrez de Lara.* Cuadernos de Historia, series 1967, no. 2. Ciudad Victoria: Ediciones Siglo XX, 1967.

Faulk, Odie B. *The Last Years of Spanish Texas, 1778–1821.* The Hague: Mouton & Co., 1964.

Fitzmorris, (Sister) Mary Angela. *Four Decades of Catholicism in*

Texas, 1820–1860. Washington: The Catholic University of America, 1926.

Fourtier, Alcée. *A History of Louisiana.* 4 vols. New York: Manzi, Joyant & Co., Successors, 1904.

Garrett, Julia Kathryn. *Green Flag over Texas: A Story of the Last Years of Spain in Texas.* New York and Dallas: The Cordova Press, Inc., 1939.

Griffin, Charles Carroll. *The United States and the Disruption of the Spanish Empire, 1810–1822: A Study of the Relations of the United States with Spain and with the Rebel Spanish Colonies.* New York: Columbia University Press, 1937.

Jarratt, Rie. *Gutiérrez de Lara, Mexican-Texan: The Story of a Creole Hero.* Austin: Creole Texana, 1949.

Johnson, Frank W. *A History of Texas and Texans.* Edited by Eugene C. Barker and Ernest William Winkler. 5 vols. Chicago and New York: The American Historical Society, 1916.

Loomis, Noel M., and Abraham P. Nasatir. *Pedro Vial and the Roads to Santa Fe.* Norman: University of Oklahoma Press, 1967.

Malone, Dumas, and Basil Rauch. *The Republic Comes of Age, 1789–1841.* New York: Appleton-Century-Crofts, 1960.

Maverick, Maury (cooperating sponsor). *Old Villita.* Compiled and written by the Writers' Project of the Works Projects Administration in the State of Texas. San Antonio: City of San Antonio and The Clegg Co., 1939.

Morfi, Juan Agustín. *History of Texas, 1673–1779.* Translated by Carlos Eduardo Castañeda. 2 vols. Albuquerque: The Quivira Society, 1935.

Navarro García, Luis. *Don José de Gálvez y la Comandancia General de las Provincias Internas del Norte de Nueva España.* Seville: Escuela de Estudios Hispano-Americanos de Sevilla, 1964.

―――. *Las Provincias Internas en el siglo XIX.* Seville: Escuela de Estudios Hispano-Americanos de Sevilla, 1965.

Nixon, Pat Ireland. *The Medical Story of Early Texas: 1528–1853.* Lancaster: Mollie Bennett Lupe Memorial Fund, 1946.

Pereyra, Carlos (comp.). *Obras de D. Lucas Alamán: Historia de Méjico.* 5 vols. Mexico City: Editorial Jus, 1942.

Richardson, Rupert Norval. *The Comanche Barrier to South Plains Settlement: A Century and a Half of Savage Resistance to the Advancing White Frontier.* Glendale, Calif.: The Arthur H. Clark Company, 1933.

———. *Texas: The Lone Star State.* New York: Prentice-Hall, Inc., 1943.

Sturmberg, Robert (comp.). *History of San Antonio and of the Early Days in Texas.* San Antonio: Standard Printing Co., 1920.

A Twentieth Century History of Southwest Texas. 2 vols. Chicago: The Lewis Publishing Company, 1907.

Warren, Harris Gaylord. *The Sword Was Their Passport: A History of American Filibustering in the Mexican Revolution.* Baton Rouge: Louisiana State University Press, 1943.

Webb, Walter Prescott (ed.). *The Handbook of Texas.* 2 vols. Austin: The Texas State Historical Association, 1952.

———. *The Texas Rangers: A Century of Frontier Defense.* Boston: Houghton Mifflin Company, 1935.

Yoakum, H[enderson R.] *History of Texas: From Its First Settlement in 1685 to Its Annexation to the United States in 1846.* 2 vols. New York: J. S. Redfield, 1855. Reprinted., 2 vols. in one, Austin: The Steck Company, n. d.

ARTICLES AND PERIODICALS

Austin, Mattie Alice. "The Municipal Government of San Fernando de Bexar, 1739–1800." *Quarterly of the Texas State Historical Association* 8, no. 4 (April, 1905): 277–352.

Benson, Nettie Lee (ed. and trans.). "A Governor's Report on Texas in 1809." *Southwestern Historical Quarterly* 71, no. 4 (April, 1968): 603–615.

———. "Bishop Marín de Porras and Texas." *Southwestern Historical Quarterly* 51, no. 1 (July, 1947): 16–40.

———. "Texas Failure to Send a Deputy to the Spanish Cortes, 1810–1812." *Southwestern Historical Quarterly* 64, no. 1 (July, 1960): 14–35.

Bolton, Herbert Eugene. "Defensive Spanish Expansion and Significance of the Borderlands." In *Bolton and the Spanish Border-*

lands, edited by John Francis Bannon. Norman: University of Oklahoma Press, 1964.

Brooks, Philip C. "Spain's Farewell to Louisiana, 1803–1821." *Mississippi Valley Historical Review* 27, no. 1 (June, 1940): 29–40.

Carroll, H. Bailey (ed.). "Texas Collection: Governors of Texas, 1778–1822." *Southwestern Historical Quarterly* 66, no. 4 (April, 1963): 593–594.

Cox, Isaac Joslin. "The Louisiana-Texas Frontier." *Southwestern Historical Quarterly* 17, nos. 1 and 2 (July, October, 1913): 1–42, 140–187.

———. "The Louisiana-Texas Frontier during the Burr Conspiracy." *Mississippi Valley Historical Review* 10, no. 3 (December, 1923): 274–284.

Crimmins, M. L. "Augustus William Magee, the Second Advance Courier of American Expansion to Texas." *West Texas Historical Association Year Book* 20 (October, 1944): 92–99.

Faulk, Odie B. "Ranching in Spanish Texas." *Hispanic American Historical Review* 45, no. 2 (May, 1965): 257–266.

Fisher, Lillian E. "American Influence upon the Movement for Mexican Independence." *Mississippi Valley Historical Review* 18, no. 4 (March, 1932): 463–478.

Garrett, [Julia] Kathryn. "The First Constitution of Texas, April 17, 1813." *Southwestern Historical Quarterly* 40, no. 4 (April, 1937): 290–308.

———. "The First Newspaper of Texas: Gaceta de Texas." *Southwestern Historical Quarterly* 40, no. 3 (January, 1937): 200–215.

Haggard, J. Villasana. "The Counter-Revolution of Béxar, 1811." *Southwestern Historical Quarterly* 43, no. 2 (October, 1939): 222–235.

———. "The Houses of Barr and Davenport." *Southwestern Historical Quarterly* 44, no. 1 (July, 1945): 66–88.

———. "The Neutral Ground between Louisiana and Texas, 1806–1821." *Louisiana Historical Quarterly* 28, no. 4 (October, 1945): 1001–1128.

Henderson, Harry McCorry. "The Magee-Gutierrez Expedition." *Southwestern Historical Quarterly* 55, no. 1 (July, 1951): 43–61.

Houston, Virginia H. Taylor. "Surveying in Texas." *Southwestern Historical Quarterly* 45, no. 2 (October, 1961): 204–233.

Lanier, Sidney. "San Antonio de Bexar." In *San Antonio de Bexar: A Guide and History,* compiled and edited by William Corner. San Antonio: Bainbridge & Corner, 1890.

M'Caleb, Walter Flavius. "The First Period of the Gutierrez-Magee Expedition." *Quarterly of the Texas State Historical Association* 4, no. 3 (January, 1901): 218–229.

Moore, R. Woods. "The Role of the Baron de Bastrop in the Anglo-American Settlement of the Spanish Southwest." *Louisiana Historical Quarterly* 31, no. 3 (July, 1948): 606–681.

Santos, Richard G. "The Quartel de San Antonio de Bexar." *Texana* 5, no. 3 (Fall, 1967): 187–202.

Warren, Harris Gaylord. "José Álvarez de Toledo's Initiation as a Filibuster, 1811–1813." *Hispanic American Historical Review* 20, no. 1 (February, 1940): 58–82.

Webb, Walter Prescott (ed.). "Texas Collection: Christmas and New Year in Texas." *Southwestern Historical Quarterly* 44, no. 3 (January, 1941): 357–379.

INDEX

194   *Index*

Council of Regency: established, 67–
    68
Council of the Indies: appoints Sal-
    cedo governor, 24 n.
Crimmins, Martin Lalor: on Magee's
    death, 167 n.
Croix, Theodoro de: 6
Crown Infantry Regiment: 37
Cuba: 105

D'Alvimar, Octaviano: plans to revo-
    lutionize northern New Spain, 25;
    arrested, 25; Texas officials on, 26
Davenport, Samuel: allowed to enter
    Texas, 5 n.; and border security,
    61–62; reports on Salcedo's family,
    132; as interpreter, Neutral Ground
    invasion, 137
de la Garza, Felipe: reports on ill-
    ness at Trinidad, 72; command of,
    105; reports on Indian problems,
    146–147; recalled to capital, 155
de la Garza, Isidro: leads troops into
    Neutral Ground, 139–140; assigned
    to Trinidad outpost, 155
de la Rosa, Francisco: 49
Delgado, Antonio: assassinates royal-
    ists, 171; as murderer, 174
depopulation: 69, 99
deserters, army. SEE Army, U.S., de-
    serters from
Díaz de Bustamante, José Ramón:
    and travelers through Laredo, 108;
    and enlistments, 111, 116; leads
    troops to Camargo, 145; and gov-
    ernorship of Nuevo León, 146, 149,
    150; criticized, 150; and reinforce-
    ments for Salcedo, 150, 157; Sal-
    cedo on promotion of, 152–153;
    mentioned, 148, 153, 160
Dolores: Hidalgo revolt at, 76, 77;
    revolt spreads from, 95
Domínguez, Cristóbal: inspects the
    troops, 70; oversees Texas defense,
    103; reestablishes royalist rule in
    Nacogdoches, 124; transferred to
    Rio Grande, 125–126; sends troops
    to Béxar, 138, 144; and Indian
    raids, 144, 145; and defense of Ca-
    margo, 145–146; and reinforce-
    ments for Salcedo, 157, 165; to
    Monclova, 161; as Texas governor,
    182; mentioned, 100
Durango: 101

East Texas: defense of, 17, 33, 35, 64,
    68, 131, 148; Neutral Ground in,
    17–18; contraband trade in, 26;
    fugitive slaves in, 28–29; U.S.
    army deserters in, 29–30; horses in,
    40–41; tensions in, regarding al-
    iens, 42; revolt rumored in, 55, 68–
    69; emigration from, 69, 98, 99;
    mail service to, 82; effects of Hi-
    dalgo revolt in, 98; inhabitants of,
    restricted, 108; Salcedo's family to,
    115; insurrections in, 119; Gutié-
    rrez propaganda in, 148, 153, 155;
    and Gutiérrez-Magee expedition,
    159. SEE ALSO Nacogdoches
elections. SEE municipal elections
Elizondo, Ignacio: allegiance of, 119,
    121–122; actions of, against Hidalgo
    army, 122; and defense of Camar-
    go, 145; assists commandant gen-
    eral, 175; battles Gutiérrez forces,
    175–176; defeated, 176; at Battle
    of Medina, 178–179
émigrés, Hispanic: invited to return
    to Texas, 69; resettle in Texas, 74;
    arrest of, ordered, 98
epsom salts: 87
escribano: need for, 38; employed by
    Salcedo, 80, 102
Espíritu Santo Bay: 164
excommunication: of Salcedo, 93–94

farming: 18–19
Ferdinand VII: 65, 95, 121
filibusters. SEE Álvarez de Toledo,
    José Antonio; Gutiérrez de Lara,
    Bernardo; Gutiérrez-Magee expe-
    dition; Long, James; Magee, Au-
    gustus William; Mina, Francisco
    Xavier; Perry, Henry; Shaler,
    William
finances: of presidial companies, 48–
    49, 154–155; for East Texas de-
    fense, 58–59, 64; for war fund, 68;
    for bureaucracy, 78, 79; for hos-
    pital, 85, 87; for Mexican inde-
    pendence, 95–96; for purchase of
    armaments, 100, 102, 107, 128–129,
    149; sought for provincial treasury,
    131
Flores, José: 80
Flores, Vicente: 165
Fort Claiborne: 23, 56, 57, 114
fortifications, Spanish. SEE presidios